CONTENTS

A WORKBOOK AND GUIDE FOR

COMMITMENT

KEY TO CHRISTIAN MATURITY

Designed and developed by
Susan Muto and Adrian van Kaam
with Susan McBride

Paulist Press ■ *New York* ■ *Mahwah, N.J.*

ISBN: 0-8091-3189-7

Published by Paulist Press
997 Macarthur Boulevard
Mahwah, NJ 07430

Printed and bound in the
United States of America

PREFACE

The author Henry David Thoreau suggested in his masterful journal *Walden* that it is one thing to dream our dreams and another to put realistic foundations under them. By comparison, we can imagine how wonderful it would be to respond faithfully to our life call, to be committed to our goals of love and service, to sense the sacredness of every person, event, and thing. However lofty these Christian ideals may be, they need to be realized in the concrete kinds of practices we have sought to outline in this guide to our book: *Commitment: Key to Christian Maturity*.

We have found that lack of commitment—ranging from an inability to start a task, and complete it, to instances of gross marital infidelity—abounds in our culture. This topic has become a central issue in workshops and seminars we have conducted for diocesan clergy and religious, lay formation groups of many different ages and locations, military chaplains, and university students.

We are happy to have had the opportunity, thanks to our publisher, Paulist Press, to develop a companion to our initial thoughts on this theme in the form of a "formation guide," designed to deepen personal reflection and enhance group interaction. We are grateful to our colleague, Dr. Susan McBride, for the expertise in the field of instructional media she has brought to this project.

We believe that the joining of the original book and its companion guide will facilitate immensely the graced capacity in each of us to make a commitment and carry it through to completion as well as to appraise those commitments that must undergo renewal and change. We trust that our efforts will be rewarded by the spiritual progress each reader can make toward being and becoming spiritually mature. With the help of God's ever present and sustaining grace, we may be at the beginning of a new era of commitment in the western world.

Dr. Susan Muto
Father Adrian van Kaam
January 1990

INTRODUCTION

For years, Dr. Adrian van Kaam and Dr. Susan Muto have been guiding people seeking to grow in Christian maturity. Some twenty-five years ago, Dr. van Kaam founded the Institute of Formative Spirituality at Duquesne University, a graduate department that grants advanced degrees in formation science. Dr. Muto, a colleague of his for over twenty years, served as the Institute's director from 1980 to 1988.

During the time of academic commitment, both came to see a growing need and desire among adult Christian laity for solid spiritual formation. Ten years ago, to begin to meet that need, Father Adrian and Susan co-founded the Epiphany Association, an ecumenical formation center for laity in the Pittsburgh area as well as a research, publication, and resource center, pledged to sharing worldwide the collected wisdom of formative spirituality.

In 1988 Dr. Muto became executive director of the Epiphany Association so that the center could more dedicatedly serve the many requests being received for sound spiritual guidance. In addition to their continuing publications, books, lectures, workshops, and seminars, which they have delivered locally, nationally, and internationally, these two persons are branching out to make other media resources available. As an expert in instructional design and development, it has been my honor to consult with Father Adrian and Susan on this formation guide, which complements their book, *Commitment: Key to Christian Maturity*.

We have developed this guide for persons using the *Commitment* text for self-direction and also those using it for direction-in-common by means of small study groups. Both forms of direction are identified and explained by van Kaam in his classic work entitled *The Dynamics of Spiritual Self-Direction* (Denville, N.J.: Dimension Books, 1976). The guide is organized in such a way as to facilitate the formative reading of the book and to nurture spiritual deepening. It is designed to help us better integrate what we believe and how we live, our faith and our daily formation, our choices and our life call.

In addition to this formation guide, I am currently working with the Epiphany Association, under the personal direction of Dr. van Kaam and

Dr. Muto, on two other media-related projects. First, we are collaborating on an audio accompaniment to this book, which will also be released by Paulist Press. Second, we are developing and will be producing an innovative six-part video series. The program, which deals with becoming spiritually mature, will draw upon and present in an inspiring, visual way the wisdom of formative spirituality originated by Father van Kaam.

We trust that this particular book and the formation guide accompanying it will enhance each individual's sense of commitment to Christ and encourage lasting fidelity to one's divine life call.

Susan D. McBride, Ph.D.

OVERVIEW

Formation is an ever ongoing process. Like our breathing it never stops. From birth to death, we both receive form from and give form to our life and world. As human beings we are called to give a spiritual direction to this formation story. As Christians we are empowered by grace to receive the Christ form in our hearts and to radiate this form into our life and world.

Through a variety of means, this *Workbook and Guide for Commitment: Key to Christian Maturity* helps us to reflect on the concrete reality of commitment, to see it as a key for unlocking the doors to grace prompting our Christian formation journey. Like the apostle, Paul, we, too, must "press on toward the goal for the prize of the upward call of God in Christ Jesus. Let those of us who are mature be thus minded; and if in anything you are otherwise minded, God will reveal that also to you. Only let us hold true to what we have attained" (Phil 3:14–16; RSV).

INTENDED AUDIENCE

This guide is primarily for lay individuals and groups who have been spiritually awakened, perhaps through one of many renewal movements, and are now asking, "Where do we go from here?" It is for those of us who want to grow in the Spirit, not outside, but inside, our secular activities, who have asked, "How can we, as committed lay Christians, practice spirituality?"

This guide is for anyone who has come to know that spiritual growth does not end at some "magical moment" called adulthood. As scripture confirms, it is a process of formation, reformation, and graced transformation that occurs over a lifetime. We are continually becoming new creations, for, as Paul says, "We all, with unveiled face, beholding the glory of the Lord, are being changed into his likeness from one degree of glory to another; for this comes from the Lord who is the Spirit" (2 Cor 3:18; RSV).

FORMATIVE APPROACH

A formative approach inclines us to ask how the life direction revealed by Christ can grace and illumine the ever ongoing movement of formation within our everyday world. This formation guide serves us in doing that. Any individual may benefit from using the guide, but it is also meant to encourage small group interaction. The Holy Spirit can and does use a text of scripture or of the spiritual masters to disclose formation directives in our here and now situation. He inspires thoughts, motivations, images, and symbols that point us to the direction our life formation should take. In a similar way the Spirit can and does use small groups to awaken reflective insights we could never discover alone.

Having small groups that meet regularly for spiritual growth is more and more coming to be seen as vital to Christian life. As Jesus told the groups he directed, "Where two or three are gathered together in my name, there am I in the midst of them" (Mt 18:20; NAB). Christ expressed clearly that Christianity is about relationship—our relationship with God, self, and others. Insofar as we are one body in Christ, inter-formative encounters become avenues through which the Spirit addresses our hearts.

There is an increasing trend among Christians to be involved in several diverse Christian gatherings, as we seek to broaden our spiritual understanding and to see from a wider perspective the meaning of being "one in Christ Jesus" (Gal 3:28; NAB). While remaining active in and loyal to our own local congregations and without compromising our own faith and formation traditions, we Christians are becoming involved in ecumenical groups in our schools, communities, and places of work.

Faith traditions give the basic content of our faith, as interpreted by the church to which we are committed. These are studied by theology. Formation traditions contain the varied ways in which we, as Christians or adherents of other faith traditions, try to live our faith in our own practical everyday here and now world. Formation science and its Christian articulation explores these ways.

The Epiphany Center was itself established under the aegis of a formative ecumenical vision that first and foremost fosters in people a commitment to their own tradition; secondarily it helps them identify commonalities typical of human nature as spiritual and, for Christians, commonalities found in basic spiritual formation directives disclosed in scripture and the writings of spiritual masters.

It follows that this guide has been developed to support a significant trend and to be a resource for any small group gathering. The text takes to heart the words of Paul: ". . . we all attain to the unity of the faith and the knowledge of the Son of God to mature personhood, to the measure of the stature of the fullness of Christ; so that we may no longer be children, tossed to and fro and carried about with every wind of doctrine, by the cunning of men, by their craftiness in deceitful wiles. Rather, speaking the truth in love, we are to grow up in every way into him who is the head, into Christ, from whom the whole body, joined and knit together by every joint with which it is supplied, when each part is working properly, makes bodily growth and upbuilds itself in love" (Eph 4:13–16; RSV).

This guide fosters formative direction-in-common. That means it encourages a shared exploration. What is it that we can explore with our brothers and sisters in Christ? Tapping into the spiritual insights of two formation experts, we can share our attempts to understand and unfold the basic spiritual direction of our always ongoing formation in the light of scripture and the classical masters of Christian formation. As a way of faith deepening, such an approach has to be preceded, completed, and corrected by personal formative direction in light of one's own church affiliation and personal life call.

CONTENTS OF THE GUIDE

This resource consists of six divisions that parallel the six parts of *Commitment: Key to Christian Maturity*. Titles and chapters for these are given below. Also provided is a goal statement that summarizes the guide's reflective focus for that part of the text and allows us to see at a glance the general theme of the content.

Part 1: Living Commitment (Chapters 1, 2, and 3)
Goal: To recognize our underlying call, as laity, to be committed to God, self, and others and to explore how to live this unique call within the everyday world wherein we find ourselves.

Part 2: Commitment and the Threefold Path (Chapters 4, 5, 6, and 7)
Goal: To describe the paths of obedience, poverty of spirit, and chaste love as directives for discipleship that all are to follow.

Part 3: Love and Commitment (Chapters, 8, 9, 10, 11, 12, and 13)
Goal: To consider mature love from the viewpoint of both marriage and singleness, understood as callings to follow Christ in communion with committed others.

Part 4: Living Community (Chapters 14 and 15)
Goal: To explore the signs of a sound Christian community of committed laity and to distinguish the Spirit-inspired, graced ground from which such a gathering emerges.

Part 5: Commitment and Human Work (Chapters 16, 17, 18, 19, 20, 21, and 22)
Goal: To examine the obstacles to and the facilitating conditions for being a committed Christian presence in the workplace.

Part 6: Commitment and Prayerful Living as Laity (Chapters 23, 24, and 25)
Goal: To show that spiritual disciplines and a life of prayer nourish us and keep our lives oriented toward our deeper calling and commitment.

INTERACTION METHODS

To provide direction for both personal and group deepening, each division, in addition to the focus provided by the goal statement, includes five different learning methods. These are:

- **Return to the Message**
- **Reflect upon the Meaning**
- **Relate to Scripture**
- **Record Your Dialogue**
- **Reclaim the Classics**

Each of these ways of approaching the text helps us to take in its full richness. They invite us to see not only the immediate meaning, but to wind our way slowly down to its inner, less-quickly-seen depth and to widen our view to include its broader, more-far-reaching breadth. As singular persons using these aids to heighten our reflective ability, we should move through them slowly at our own comfortable, unrushed pace.

The first three methods are layered in a spiral fashion, so they are best approached consecutively. *Return to the Message* focuses; *Reflect upon the Meaning* deepens; and *Relate to Scripture* widens our vision. Although most beneficial when completed in the sequence presented, these three are not intended to be used all at one time, in a single sitting. We should come to each one at different, perhaps even several, times, when using them for our own spiritual formation.

If we are also part of a group, agreed-to procedural and time guidelines, such as those outlined in this guide under the subheading *"For Setting up a Group,"* will have been established for our sessions together from the very beginning. This helps us to know what amount of material the group plans to include for any single session. Knowing this, we can come already prepared to offer our insights on a few of the things that spoke most strongly to us.

It is not the intent of such a schedule, nor should it become the practice, to regiment or mechanize the interaction of the group. The purpose of having a set sequence of events with recommended time limits is simply to provide clarity via a shared, comfortable framework that invites participation and facilitates the flow of the interaction.

The last two methods should be approached in yet another way since they are more for personal than group use. *Record Your Dialogue* may be done at any time while dwelling on a particular part of the text. *Reclaim the Classics* is best considered as a closing activity, just before one moves into the next part of the original text and formation guide combination.

Return to the Message

This method provides another structural or organizational framework for considering central insights presented in the original text. Remaining consistent with the sequential flow of chapters, *Return to the Message* directs our attention to different key words or phrases for each of the six parts. Each of these is followed by clarifying statements. Key words or phrases for each of the six parts are as follows:

Part 1: Living Commitment

Our Unique Call ● Risk of Commitment ● Seeking Direction ● Awe-Filled Faith ● Living in Fidelity ● Choices and Limits ● Seduction as an Obstacle ● Appeal as an Invitation ● From Commitment to Consecration ● Divine Depth of Our Call ● Messages of Divine Providence ● Trust in God's Grace ● Mark of Christian Maturity.

Part 2: Commitment and the Threefold Path

The Threefold Path ● Obedience ● Readiness ● Willingness ● Respectful Dialogue ● Poverty of Spirit ● Possessiveness ● Gifts from God ● Detachment or Daily Distancing ● Poverty of Being ● In the Light of Hope ● Jesus' Way of Poverty ● Chaste Love ● Healing Power of the Threefold Path.

Part 3: Love and Commitment

Marital Intimacy and Commitment ● Directives for Marriage ● Reality of Marriage ● Romantic Experience ● Sacramental Commitment ● Dispositions of Committed Love ● Fallacies of Romantic Love ● Integration of Sexuality and Spirituality ● From Self-Centered to Other-Centered Love ● Singleness as Consecration.

Part 4: Living Community

Crowd ● Collectivity ● Formation Community ● Congeniality ● Compatibility ● Compassion ● Courage ● Competence ● Humanistic Community ● Pneumatic Community ● Spirit-Inspired Capacity ● Affinity of Grace ● Moments of Renewed Inspiration.

Part 5: Commitment and Human Work

Split in Christian Consciousness ● Effects of the Split ● Integration of Work and Spirituality ● Functionalism ● Functionalism and the Threefold Path ● Homogeneity and Alienation ● Specialization ● Specialization and the Threefold Path ● Cultural Obstacles to Commitment ● Committed Christian Presence ● Erosion and Depletion ● Appraisal Disposition ● Conditions Reforming and Facilitating Christian Presence ● Repletion Sessions.

Part 6: Commitment and Prayerful Living as Laity
Daily Deepening ● Spiritual Frigidity ● Overcoming Spiritual Frigidity ● Avenues to Committed Living ● Formative or Spiritual Reading ● Dispositions Fostering Receptivity ● Knowing with the Heart ● Seeing in Faith ● Remaining Simple in a Complex World ● Practice of Prayer ● Prayer of Presence ● Moments of Stillness.

Reading over these on our own helps us to refocus formatively on the distinctive spiritual truths presented for our consideration. We use this opportunity as a time to sit and be with the message, to ponder further the insights for day-to-day living that the text holds for us. Rather than feeling compelled to "cover" all the items, we approach each as if we were returning to friends already made in our first reading. Using the spaces provided for our entries, we add our reflective thoughts to those offered in the guide or list key words or ideas from our own spontaneous marking of the original text.

This returning to the message refreshes our memory, sparks our imagination, and increases our anticipation. It prepares us for our involvement in and commitment to a small formative study group. The actual group sharing for this *Return to the Message* is not intended to be extensive, but merely to highlight something that really spoke to us. *Reflect upon the Meaning* is given more time in the group because it provides stimulus questions that help to guide the group's direction-in-common for the insights first glimpsed in *Return to the Message.*

This prior personal reflection, however, is most important in one's commitment to being part of a group. It eases the singular responsibility of a group leader per se and facilitates our own accountability in the group process. It readies us to share reflective insights with others seeking spiritual maturity in a way that can be formatively enriching for us and them.

Reflect upon the Meaning

This method includes two types of activities. First, there is an exercise to be done on our own, again at one's own leisure. It asks us to locate ourselves between two extremes of several continuums. Doing so helps to shed light on where we are in relation to some of the key insights from that part of the text, to better see possible resonances or resistances. This exercise is designed as a singular activity, to be done prior to a group session. It aims to sharpen our personal focus and facilitate insightful contributions within the group.

The second activity in *Reflect upon the Meaning* provides several discussion statements and question clusters to stimulate the depth of both personal and group thinking. These invite us to go below the level of intellectual understanding as we immerse ourselves in the text's message for our spiritual life. Working first separately, at our own comfortable pace, we reflect upon the statements and subsequent question clusters, writing, when possible, responses in the spaces provided.

This type of personal reflection serves us well when we are a member of a group. Advance preparation increases the fruits of direction-in-common through small group interaction. Using the original text in combination with this formation guide allows for a deeper level of thoughtful sharing concerning the spiritual guidance contained in *Commitment: Key to Christian Maturity*.

Relate to Scripture

This method links ideas in the original text to the spiritual wisdom contained in holy scripture. It provides scripture-based statements and question clusters to activate the breadth dimension of our thinking. Using the context of the "commitment window" as their focus, these clusters invite us to widen the book's potential for reflection and to relate to the word of God that undergirds it. Both *Return to the Message* and *Reflect upon the Meaning* prepare us for formative, thematic scripture reading.

We try to approach this reading as a humble directee seeking the grace of illumination. When we foster formative presence to the word of God, we begin to see the reality of God's self-communication to humankind in the familiar persons, events, stories, and words of scripture. We begin to discover more deeply the self we are before God.

As we first read the designated scriptures, we try to come to an inner dialogue with the Spirit speaking in the text. We seek inspiration and practical direction in our day-to-day spiritual life, rather than just obtaining interesting or scholarly information. Working separately, again at our own pace, we consider the statements and subsequent question clusters, writing responses in the spaces provided. By taking time to be with the word of God, our vision is widened. We begin to see the relevance of scripture for everyday living and to find the spiritual formation we seek.

Relate to Scripture can also be fruitfully used by groups, for any of the six parts of the *Commitment* text, should we wish an additional one or two direction-in-common sessions. Before beginning to express our insights on commitment, as stimulated by the scripture related statements and question clusters to which we have already prepared responses, it would be wise to review the group's purpose for this interaction. Like one's personal reflection, this is to be a time for inspirational, practical exchange, a time to share what nourishes and feeds us in our daily, spiritual life.

When we take this opportunity to express previously recorded or new insights, we not only facilitate the group process; but we also have an opportunity to check out the meanings and directives gathered in our own reading with other Christians disposed to spiritual growth. Reasonable validation by others of our own spontaneous formative inspirations is thus attained.

Record Your Dialogue

This learning method gives us an opportunity to personally dialogue with the whispers of the Spirit. Recording provides time for recollection and remaining in the meaning so that we personalize insights in line with our unique call. Entries may be recorded at any time as we focus separately and then communally, if we are a member of a small group, on the six different parts of the original text as enriched by this formation guide.

Keeping such a formative notebook can deepen our spiritual growth. Once written, our thoughts gain objectivity and become a text in their own right to which we can later return. Coming home to these recorded insights and inspirations over and over again reminds us of our original insights. These periodic reviews of our notebook entries often help us to see more clearly the mystery of God's directing will in daily events.

Because our notebooks are private, recordings do not have to be shared in group interactions. However, if we are in a group where all members are comfortable with, and favorably disposed to, a short sharing of recorded insights by those wishing to express them, time could be provided at the end of one session or the beginning of another to do so.

Reclaim the Classics

In this section, Christian classics have been selected and annotated by Father van Kaam and Dr. Muto to help us see the way in which believers throughout our history have, as the people of God, lived their call, commitment, and consecration as members of the community of the faithful. The spiritual masters of these timely and timeless classics offer irreplaceable resources for spiritual deepening. To familiarize us with some of this "hidden" treasure, the co-authors list seven texts, representing ancient, medieval, modern, and contemporary spiritual masters, for each part of the *Commitment* text. Works were chosen because they depict background reading and writing that helped in forming the *Commitment* authors' insights for that part of their original text. As we read over each list and reflect on the glimpses given, we may discover some books that call to us as future avenues for our own deepening.

Although intended primarily for individual enrichment and direction, the classics listed could be used for group study, if the group in question had a strong motivation to continue direction-in-common through spiritual reading. However, since guides for group use of these resources are not included here, it is advisable to find an experienced facilitator to help the group work through these texts in a formative way.

GUIDELINES FOR PROCEEDING

All reflection begins with a single person. Whether we complete this formation guide on our own or as a member of a small group, there are a few guidelines to keep in mind. Below are some suggestions for "getting started." They are divided into the topics:

- For the person reflecting alone
- For setting up the group
- For the group members
- For the group facilitator(s)

For the Person Reflecting Alone

Personal preparation and commitment are essential. Each separate part of the original text should be read and marked before using its complementary part in the formation guide. Spontaneous marking of the original text helps us read in a slowed down way. It keeps in our mind what "pops out" as meaningful and makes it more our own.

Questions To Consider When Reflecting on Our Own

- Is there something in this text that is relevant to my way of life?
- Do I feel resistance or resonance when reading? What is the source of these feelings?
- Do I dwell quietly on what the words seem to be telling me?
- Where and how does what I am reading tie in with my daily life?
- How can the text be assimilated by me in such a way that it animates and guides my spiritual growth here and now?

Once the original text has been read and marked, it is time to use this formation guide. If the choice has been to use it solely on one's own, personal discipline becomes key. While writing in the guide is important in preparing for a group gathering, it is even more critical when we are reflecting alone. Spending a regularly-scheduled period of time interacting with the guide and text is important, too. In summary, when reflecting alone:

Create an Inner Disposition of

- Recollected Presence
- Peaceful Expectancy
- Prayerful Receptivity

For Setting up a Group

We may have already decided that the discipline and direction of a small group is a good way to grow spiritually. Perhaps we are or have been involved in such a group through some kind of renewal program. To begin this study, we need to gather a group of similarly disposed people who are seeking the same ideal of spiritual maturity in Christ.

Set aside a period of time, convenient for all, in which to come together. Sessions may occur weekly, bi-weekly or even monthly. They may range anywhere from six to twelve sessions, depending on whether one or two sessions will be devoted to a particular part of the text.

Group size may also vary. Eight to ten is considered a good number and is conducive to exchanging a variety of insights and experiences. Small groups have been done effectively with as few as four and as many as sixteen. For deeper guidance and direction, Christ himself choose twelve, and for greater intimacy, three.

Generally small group gatherings last between forty-five and one hundred and twenty minutes. Length of time available will dictate how the meeting might proceed. What is important is for the group to meet regularly for a set time and to follow a familiar pattern with which all are comfortable.

Pattern for Ninety Minute Session Using This Formation Guide

OPENING PRAYER (1 MINUTE)
Group facilitator opens with short prayer relating to the evening's topic.

WARM UP (10 MINUTES)
Group members introduce each other (if first session or if new members are present). For later sessions, group members may express any new insights relating to the previous session.

GOAL (2 MINUTES)
Someone reads the goal being focused on for this session.

RETURN TO THE MESSAGE (15 MINUTES)
Facilitator asks for comments on the **Return to the Message** portion of the session and has participants share some words or phrases of their own.

REFLECT UPON THE MEANING (55 MINUTES)

Facilitator guides the **Reflect upon the Meaning** portion, encouraging members to share their insights. Note: If the group has decided on two sessions for this part, *Relate to Scripture* may be used for the second session.

WRAP UP (5 MINUTES)

Facilitator closes the session with suggestions for reflection between sessions, final comments, and questions.

CLOSING PRAYER (2 MINUTES)

Group facilitator closes with a short prayer of thanksgiving and praise relating to the evening's sharing and insights.

For the Group Members

As members of a small Christian group well disposed to growing spiritually, each of us must accept both personal and group responsibility for an open, honest, and trusting relationship to develop. We each need to prepare by completing, in advance of the session, the relevant portions of the original text and the formation guide.

Once assembled, all in the group are responsible for participating. Each member has unique experiences, skills, and gifts to contribute which add to the richness of the group experience. It is also crucial for participants in the group to relate, in personal, prayerful reflection, the insights gained to their own Christian tradition as well as to one's own unique life call. Complementing or correcting what deviates from these commitments is a necessary step in becoming spiritually mature. As group members who share direction-in-common, it would be wise to review the following general principles before each session.

General Principles for Group Members

- Be present in a spiritually receptive stance.
- Contribute from your own store of formative events.
- Recognize the value of all contributions and the importance of each person's originality.

- Respond to one another's contributions by thanks or other means that show genuine interest.
- Build on the contributions of others when possible rather than simply throwing in an unrelated idea.
- Summarize from time to time and highlight some of the similarities and uniquenesses in each other's spiritual journeys.
- Be open to how the Spirit may use us.
- Nurture spiritual deepening and growth by drawing others out, when appropriate.
- Encourage the personal and respectful relating of the shared insights to one's own specific Christian tradition and unique life call.
- Allow for times of silence and thought.
- Respect the confidentiality of the group sharing.

Although our intentions are usually well meaning when involved in a group interaction, at times our fallenness makes its presence known. Remaining aware of the following pitfalls to interaction and reviewing them before our group session may help in avoiding them.

Pitfalls to Interaction

- Choosing to be a critical presence
- Playing one-up-manship
- Indulging in intellectualism
- Engaging in theological debate
- Feeling obliged to fill in the silent spaces
- Not respecting each other's Christian faith and formation tradition

For the Group Facilitator(s)

Although leadership is shared as different members use their own gifts to build up the one body, each session will need a designated facilitator to guide the group through its usual pattern. This role may be filled by the same person each time, or it may be rotated among group members if desired.

By modeling Christian discipleship, this person can foster conditions that may "facilitate" the receptivity of people for grace. However, because accountability is shared, it is good if all members are sensitized to some of the dynamics of fruitful interaction.

Because God can and does speak through us to one another, it is good to recognize four elements that a facilitator should attend to when guiding the group.

Elements of Interaction

● **Participation:** How easy or how difficult does it seem for members to participate at a comfortable level? Is participation balanced or do a few tend to dominate the interaction? Is only one person talking at a time or are two or more talking at once or having side conversations?

● **Listening:** Are there signs of much or little respectful presence? Is there minimal interrupting or lots of jumping in while others are talking? Does there seem to be an open or closed posture of listening to one another? Is there a spiritual attitude of patient, humble attention or of impatience or inattentiveness?

● **Clarity of Purpose:** Does the flow of interaction generally stay with the overall theme and goal, or does it frequently wander from the topic? Is the established format generally being followed or is the pattern somewhat haphazard or chaotic?

● **Atmosphere:** Is the climate natural, informal and accepting or stiff, formal and judgmental? Is there a sense of caring and belonging, or indifference and separateness? Do honesty and trust seem present, or are they lacking?

When one is the designated facilitator for all sessions, or for even one session, if leadership is rotated, that person has a key role in enabling the group process to flow smoothly without becoming routinized. What helps in guiding the group is to genuinely see oneself in the servant role as leader. It also helps if one is prepared. Knowing the *purpose* for the evening's gathering and reviewing the pattern for our session and appropriate sections of the guide before coming will help one in being able to create a natural *atmosphere* that encourages and invites *participation.* Modeling respectful *listening* while guiding the flow can also favorably affect the group's interaction.

Being familiar with these guidelines is good for all group members for they provide a gauge or way of reading whether our group's interaction is optimal or problematic. They help us to see in what specific ways we might personally seek to help with the group facilitation. Reading over the questions for each of the elements prior to a group session and deciding to be responsible for and sensitive in our interactions in relation to them will benefit us and others in our small group gatherings.

Most important, however, in our Christian small group interaction is for each of us to be humbly open to God's grace and the inspiration of the Holy Spirit. Becoming spiritually mature requires our cooperation and participation, but it is essentially the work of God, a gift God bestows upon those who seek him. We need to have respect for the gentle and compelling movements of the Spirit among ourselves and other members of the group as we seek spiritual self-direction and direction-in-common through the use of formative reading and sharing.

REFERENCES

The following references list key works by Dr. Muto and Dr. van Kaam that expand further upon formative reading of scripture and other classic and contemporary spiritual masters. They are beneficial resources with which a person or group may wish to become familiar.

Muto, Susan Annette. *Approaching the Sacred: An Introduction to Spiritual Reading.* Denville, N.J.: Dimension Books, 1973.
    Formative reading is one means by which we can create an inner atmosphere of receptive attention to the divine directives that may be disclosed to us by the Holy Spirit in and through the writings of the masters. The author describes this art and discipline in detail and discusses some common obstacles and facilitating conditions associated with any attempt to see God's self-revelation in our here and now situation.

————. *Steps along the Way: The Path of Spiritual Reading.* Denville, N.J.: Dimension Books, 1975.

A sequel to *Approaching the Sacred,* this book offers further insight into the art and discipline of formative reading as well as presenting a lively and perceptive study of the ways men and women have struggled to find God in their daily lives: the way of unknowing, the way of imitation, the way of spiritual childhood, and the way of ceaseless prayer.

————. *The Journey Homeward: On the Road of Spiritual Reading.* Denville, N.J.: Dimension Books, 1977.
The final volume of this trilogy on spiritual reading focuses on the way in which spiritual texts trace our journey to God and enable us to relive the way others have followed. Part One considers the attitudes necessary in a person searching to come home to God. Part Two looks at what happens on the journey itself. Drawing upon the Christian classics, each chapter attempts to integrate the wisdom of the spiritual masters with everyday life experiences and concludes with a personal reflection and prayer on a text by St. John of the Cross.

————. *A Practical Guide to Spiritual Reading.* Denville, N.J.: Dimension Books, 1976.
This book fills an oft-expressed need among Christians who want to engage in regular meditative reading of scripture and the classics, but do not always know where and how to start. As a practical aid, it answers such questions as: What do I read? How can I do so more effectively? How do I distinguish between essential and edifying texts? Containing extensive biblical references and annotations of many classics, this *Practical Guide* is a must for anyone who wants to develop a formative reading program for individual or group use.

van Kaam, Adrian. *Woman at the Well.* Denville, N.J.: Dimension Books, 1976.
Using the gospel narrative of the meeting of Jesus with the Samaritan woman, the author explicates the art and discipline of meditative scripture reading. He teaches us how to be receptive to the word of grace hidden in daily events just as the Samaritan woman

discovered the hidden well of living water available to her through Christ.

————. *Looking for Jesus.* Denville, N.J.: Dimension Books, 1978.
This book offers a practical and prayerful approach to scripture reading as exemplified in the author's dialogue with the last discourse of Jesus in John's gospel. Each chapter reflects on one passage from the discourse. The reader comes to see how it is possible to derive spiritual truths and insights from approaching scripture not only informatively but formatively.

————. *The Mystery of Transforming Love.* Denville, NJ: Dimension Books.
Looking for Jesus enabled us to reflect on the first half of the last discourse of Jesus in John's gospel. The second half of this discourse is meditated upon in this follow-up volume

————. *The Music of Eternity.* South Bend, IN: Ave Maria Press, 1990.
This book is a prayerful and poetic meditation on the formative meaning of fidelity to God's will in our everyday life situations.

PART 1

Living Commitment

ADVANCE PREPARATION
Before beginning this division of the formation guide, be sure that you have read Part One, Chapters 1, 2, and 3 of the original text.

GOAL

ON YOUR OWN
Read over the goal and consider its meaning for your own life.

IN YOUR GROUP
After opening with prayer, start the session with the facilitator reading, or asking someone else to read, the goal for this gathering.

GOAL
To recognize our underlying call, as laity, to be committed to God, self, and others and to explore how to live this unique call within the everyday world wherein we find ourselves.

RETURN TO THE MESSAGE

ON YOUR OWN
Consider the following key words and phrases, relating their message to your own situation. Copy some of the related passages you spontaneously marked in the original text, using the extra space provided. Add any key words and phrases not already on the list.

IN YOUR GROUP
As the facilitator guides this portion of your small group session, offer your thoughts on some of the words and phrases that were especially meaningful to you.

1. *Our Unique Life Call*

- We often take for granted our underlying call to be committed to God, self, and others.
- It is a call to live in faithfulness within the everyday world wherein we find ourselves; it is an invitation to grow in commitment to the tasks to which Father, Son and Holy Spirit call us uniquely.
- This unique life call beckons us to a journey of discovery, for what it entails is never fully known.

Your Thoughts:

2. *Risk of Commitment*

• The consequences of commitment reach beyond what we can foresee; they involve uncertainty.

• Even when we come to know our call, its implications will still exceed our grasp.

• Commitment threatens us because we cannot control that to which we should be committed; yet not to commit our lives to our unique life call, as lived in communion with others, is to risk living a meaningless existence.

Your Thoughts:

_____

3. *Seeking Direction*

• Each step along the way of our call to commitment reveals something more about the mosaic of our life.

• At privileged moments, the Holy Spirit may grant us some disclosure of the pointing of providence.

• There is a thread of meaning, a mysterious direction, to the strange detours of our journey.

• We stand, fascinated and fearful, on the sacred ground of knowing we must commit our lives to what God wants for us, even though this "what" remains mysterious.

Your Thoughts:

4. Awe-Filled Faith

- We must bow in awe before the mystery of our deepest life call and live in the darkness of faith.
- Faith is an attitude of readiness to respond to the unexpected, a willingness to harmonize our response to fresh challenges with our formation up to now.
- In faith, we remain ready to behold events as pointers to a wider meaning while trusting the calling Trinity in the everyday events that make up our life.

Your Thoughts:

---

5. Living in Fidelity

- Fidelity is the firm yet flexible disposition of heart and mind which enables us to remain faithful.
- This disposition generates a heightened sensitivity to any disclosure of life's design the Spirit may grant us.
- To be faithful to our commitments is to participate as Christians in the process of calling humanity back to its spiritual purpose.

Your Thoughts:

6. Choices and Limits

● As we become aware of our call, we are free to accept or reject what is asked of us.

● Time and again we must seek to choose the direction of our lives in light of our divine calling.

● Following the call to commit our lives in one direction necessarily limits our availability to move in another.

● Saying yes to what is true to our life call and having the courage to say no to what is not true is a risk worth taking—but there are obstacles along the way.

Your Thoughts:

_____

7. Seduction as an Obstacle

● At times the temptation to be or do something unfaithful to our call can be seductive.

● We can become fascinated or "fastened" to a seducer's promised ends, to a fast road to gratification which ultimately proves unsatisfying.

● Seduction does not direct itself to our spiritual depths but addresses only partial, periodical, and mundane needs painted as the whole picture.

Your Thoughts:

8. *Appeal as Invitation*

- Appeal is an invitation that moves us as spirit and touches the unique, relatively free Christ-form of our soul; it is the Spirit's appeal to commit ourselves in a certain way.
- The moment of insight into the divine direction of our baptized life implies and transcends logical considerations.
- It does not play on passions for pleasure, power and possession, nor does it seduce us to move in self-centered directions; what is appealed to is that in us which is personal, free, and responsible.

Your Thoughts:

---

9. *From Commitment to Consecration*

- Grace elevates the appeal of commitment to that of a call to consecration, to oneness with the transforming will of God.
- Consecration grants human commitments a divinely inspired complement; it encompasses and elevates human motives to the realm of graced aspirations and inspirations.
- In and through Christ, life with its sufferings and joys becomes a kind of eucharist; our ordinary lives become an offering of sacrificial love to the Father in the Spirit of Jesus.
- Human life cannot hope to reach its fullness and splendor if we refuse to move with God's grace from commitment to consecration.

Your Thoughts:

10. Divine Depth of Our Call

● Our life call is a mystery, the depth of which none of us can ever penetrate; it is the Spirit's way of beckoning us out of pride and confusion to a commitment to serve God and others in this world.

● Because it has to do with our existence as a whole, it surpasses each transient and particular situation in which we find ourselves.

● Heeding the divine depth of our life direction demands openness to its past, present, and future manifestations; awareness of it depends on our level of trust in God.

Your Thoughts:

---

11. Messages of Divine Providence

● The more our spiritual life progresses, the more we are able to behold life as a pattern of providential events.

● When we stand back and view our whole course at moments of recollection, we see that what is being woven by the divine hand is in dialogue with the gifts and goals evoked by our successive life situations.

● We come to know in the face of obstacles and temptations, in pain and suffering, that "All shall be well"; we come to believe that everything that happens to us has some significance beyond what we see at first glance.

Your Thoughts:

12. Trust in God's Grace

● The Spirit invites our creative cooperation with God's loving plan for humanity and the world.

● Trust in the Spirit tells us that what is happening is not merely a crisis, a moment of suffering, a prolonged moment of pain, but also a new possibility.

● The choice before us is to treat crisis either as a time of closure because of fear or as openness because of faith.

● Jesus cannot compel this act of trust; it is ours to make in a free response to grace.

Your Thoughts:

_____

13. Mark of Christian Maturity

● To face courageously the shadows of pain and fear, to know that there is light at the end of even the darkest tunnel, is a mark of Christian maturity.

● The call to commitment and consecration beckons us to behold the sacred significance of every person, thing, or event.

● In the process of turning to God, we discover deep within our hearts the gifts of courage and competence; we sense that we are becoming God's instruments.

Your Thoughts:

_____

Other Key Words and Phrases:

REFLECT UPON THE MEANING

ON YOUR OWN
Complete the following exercise. Where would you locate yourself between the two extremes for each of the following continuums? Put an X at the place representing you at this time in your spiritual life. Reflect on why you are at this point, and consider if this is an area in which you could benefit by being open to spiritual growth.

EXERCISE ON YOUR OWN:

1. |_____|

See myself as uniquely   See myself as
called by God   "thrown" into
                                          existence

2. |_____|

Total trust   Total need
in God's plan   to be in
for my life   control of
                                          my life

3. |_____|

Totally able to   Only able to see
see life as a   life as a haphazard
pattern of   collection
providential events   of accidental or
                                          coincidental
                                          happenings

4. |_____|

In faith treat   In fear treat
crisis as time of   crisis as time
openness   of closure

ON YOUR OWN

Reflect upon the following discussion statements and subsequent question clusters. Then write your responses in the space provided. To enhance your grasp of this aspect of self-direction, you may want to refer to the original text or the *Return to the Message* section of this guide.

IN YOUR GROUP

As the facilitator guides this portion of the session, try to offer some personal reflections on the questions.

DISCUSSION STATEMENTS AND QUESTION CLUSTERS FOR DEPTH:

1. **Commitment is defined as a pledge or a promise. In their title, the authors identify commitment as the key to Christian maturity. They contrast a lasting commitment with commitments that are transitory.**

   a. What do you mean when you say you've made a lasting commitment to someone or something?

   b. What are three to five of the things or people to which you are most deeply committed?

   c. What does living out your commitment to those things or people look like in your everyday life? Give examples.

d.   Why are these your most important commitments?

2.   **The authors begin Part 1 by pointing out that we often take for granted "our underlying call to be committed to God, self, and others," that we forget "the undercurrent of commitment that carries us."**

   a.   Why do the authors refer to it as an "underlying" call? Whom do they define as the "caller" or the one who has called us by name?

   b.   As a Christian, what does it mean to you "to be called"? To what does our call invite us? How is your call different from anyone else's? How is it linked to your unique identity in God?

   c.   In what way is this call an "undercurrent of commitment that carries us"? How is this undercurrent of commitment foundational to all the commitments that flow from it? How is it "behind" our lived out commitments of everyday life?

d. Why does this call to commitment hold the key to our Christian maturity, to our living out our call and being and becoming who we most deeply are in God?

3. **The authors tell us that commitment is a risk; yet our call to commitment continues to beckon.**

   a. What are the different reasons the authors give for why our call to commitment is a risk?

   b. Which reasons speak most strongly to your own life, to your own experience? Give an example that illustrates a time when you experienced your call to commitment as a risk in some way, or a time when you first realized that you are not ultimately in control.

   c. What other reasons, if any, come to mind for why our call to commitment may be seen as risky?

d. What does it mean when something beckons? What do the authors suggest makes our call to commitment beckoning? Who does the beckoning? What are we beckoned to do? In what ways have you experienced the beckoning of your own call to commitment?

4. **Our life call is a mystery that is disclosed to us over a lifetime, often in the form of appeals. Discovering its direction involves both choices and limits.**

    a. In what way is the direction of our life call disclosed or made known? How is choice involved in our life call? Why does it take courage to "say yes" to our call? In what way does following our call to commitment necessitate limits?

    b. How do you know when you are not in tune with your unique life call? What clues you in when you are on the wrong course?

    c. Recall any times when the Holy Spirit granted you some disclosure of the pointing of providence, some moments when you saw a glimpse of the path along which your life call was leading you? What was made clear to you? How was it made clear? How have these glimpses helped you to proceed on the path God has set for you?

d. Consider how the authors explain seduction. How is seduction an obstacle? What about it fascinates? In what way is it only partial, periodical, or mundane? What are some of the "seductions" that you recognize as obstacles in your own life?

e. How do the authors define an appeal? Who makes the appeal? How does it differ from seduction? In what way have you personally experienced such an appeal?

5. **The authors stress the importance of faith and fidelity in relation to our call to commitment.**

a. Define what having faith means to you. In what ways are faith and trust similar? What are the things or persons in which you have or place your faith?

b. What is the role of faith in relation to our life call to commitment? Why are we able to rest in the faith that God is always calling? What is he calling us to?

c. What does it mean to you to be faithful to something or someone? What do having faith and being faithful have in common?

d. In what way are commitment and fidelity similar? What does being faithful to your "underlying call to commitment" mean in your life? Recall a time when it was necessary to remain faithful to that call in the midst of obstacles. What was the situation? What was the outcome? What does it mean to participate in calling humanity back to its spiritual purpose?

6. **The authors suggest that our call to commitment is also a call to consecration, which is made possible in and through grace.**

a. What does the word consecration mean to you? In what context are you most familiar with the word? What enables us to commit ourselves in a consecrated way?

b. In what way is lifting our life call from commitment to a level of consecration related to growing in spiritual maturity? What does it mean to become mature as a Christian? With what do you associate eucharist? How can our lives become a kind of eucharist?

c. Heeding the divine depth of our life call is one dynamic that the authors suggest facilitates our growth, through God's grace, from commitment to consecration. What does it mean to do that? What do we often try to do instead?

d. Another dynamic facilitating consecration of our life call is heeding the messages of divine providence. What does it mean to do that? In what way are our freedom of choice and cooperation a part of this?

7. **The authors close by describing a mark of Christian maturity as "facing courageously the shadows of pain and fear, knowing that there is light at the end of even the darkest tunnel."**

a. In what way might this be a mark of Christian maturity? What does it suggest about the spiritual journey? What does it mean to become God's instruments?

b. How do you characteristically respond in times of life's inevitable crises like the death of a loved one, loss of a job, or serious illness? What meaning could there possibly be in suffering? In what way is our freedom related to the way we respond?

c. Can you think of a time in your life when your direction seemed so obscure that you had only the light at the end of the tunnel to sustain you? What was happening in your life then? What kept you going? Were there any disclosures concerning your life call that became clearer to you after this time?

d. The authors point out that "we must bow in awe before the mystery and live in the darkness of faith." Why do the authors call it the darkness of faith? What does bowing in awe before the mystery mean to you? What would or does living that way in your everyday life look like? What makes that kind of living possible for us?

RELATE TO SCRIPTURE

ON YOUR OWN
Read the scriptures from your Bible. Then write down your responses to the questions for each of the selections, using the context of the "commitment window" provided by this part of the guide.

IN YOUR GROUP
As the facilitator uses the focus passages and questions to guide the session, take the opportunity to express the spontaneous insights you have received. Be sure to have your Bibles with you so that you can refer to specific passages more easily.

SCRIPTURE STATEMENTS AND QUESTION CLUSTERS FOR BREADTH:

1. **This first set of scripture passages focuses on a biblical person familiar to us all. We will look at Abraham's unique life call through the window of commitment.**

   a. Read Genesis 12:1–9. These passages tell us about God first calling Abraham. In verse 3, notice how far the implications of God's call of Abraham extend. Note his age when starting out. Think of yourself setting out anew into an unknown place. What risks described in the *Commitment* text does Abraham face?

   b. Read Genesis 15:1–6. What part does faith play in Abraham's call?

c. Read Hebrews 11:8–11. What additional insights about Abraham's faith does this New Testament author provide?

d. Read Galatians 3:6–9. What important implication of Abraham's call does Paul bring out in this letter?

e. Read Romans 4:16–21. Reflect on how the apostle Paul describes Abraham's faith in these lines. What do they say to you personally?

f. Read Acts 3:25. How did the implications of Abraham's call exceed his grasp? Reflect on how you are heir to God's promises.

2. **Our original goal for Part 1, "Living Commitment," was "To recognize our underlying call, as laity, to be committed to God, self, and others and to explore how to live this unique call within the everyday world wherein we find ourselves." It is through this focus that we will relate to our second scriptural person: Ruth.**

a. Read Ruth 1:1–22. Consider in this passage how Ruth's call beckoned her to a journey of discovery. Comment on how she had the freedom to accept or reject her call. Reflect upon the words she speaks in verses 16 and 17 where she accepts her call. What do these verses reveal to you about Ruth?

b. Read Ruth 2:1–10. What were some of the risks these verses show that Ruth faced by following her life call?

c. Read Ruth 2:11–22; 3:1–18; 4:1–17. Reflect on the everyday-ness of Ruth's life. Trace how her direction was revealed each step of the way. How did Ruth demonstrate her faith and fidelity? Describe God's providential care for her life. What message does this contain for your own life?

d. Read Ruth 4:17 and Matthew 1:5. Relate how the implication of Ruth's call exceeded her grasp. What does this suggest to you about your own life?

3. **The third familiar person to whom we will relate is David. His unique call from God and his response to it within the Hebrew community are filled with wisdom for living.**

a. Read 1 Samuel 16:1–13. David was called and anointed by Samuel at a young age. Why does God intend for us to know about David's call before David himself knows? What does this suggest to us about the mystery of our own life call? In verse 7, what in David does God find acceptable? In verse 13, what gift did David receive from God when he was called? From whom and in what way have we also received this gift?

b. Read 2 Samuel 7:1–29. What is God's promise to David that the prophet Nathan reveals? Meditate upon David's prayer in verses 18–29. How does he respond to God's revealing of providence? What gave David the courage to pray this way? Recall a time in your life when you may have offered a similar kind of prayer. What was the situation?

c. Read Acts 2:29–36 and Acts 13:22–23. What about the implications of David's call does Peter first show us in Acts 2? How is this echoed again by Paul in Acts 13?

d. Read Revelation 5:5 and Revelation 22:16. How do these passages show a relationship between David's call and Christ?

4. **Paul's own call to preach to the Gentiles was an exceptional one. It resulted in many inspired letters that are rich with messages to ponder. The following passages, taken from a few of these letters, relate to our being called.**

   a. Read 1 Corinthians 1:1–3 and Romans 1:1–7. Paul describes his own call as well as ours. To what does he say we are called? How does this call relate to becoming spiritually mature?

   b. Read Colossians 3:15–17. These wonderful verses add another nuance to our call. To what does it say we are called? Reflect deeply on what those words say to you personally about your own life call. What is their message to you?

   c. Read Ephesians 4:1–6. What new aspect to our life call is added by these verses?

   d. Read Galatians 5:13–14. How does this call to freedom relate to the message the authors give in the *Commitment* text? What is it we are free to become?

e. Read Romans 8:28–31. Romans 8:28 is a much quoted verse from scripture. Why do you think so many people quote it? In what situations would you envision them doing so? Reflect on what these three verses say to you. What personal message do they have?

RECORD YOUR DIALOGUE

ON YOUR OWN
Record that which touches your life, that which inspires you and deepens your awareness of your life direction in the light of your commitment to your own specific Christian faith and formation tradition.

IN THE GROUP
If your group has decided to allot a short time for notebook sharing, you may, if you wish, offer insights that might benefit the other members of the group.

RECLAIM THE CLASSICS

Read over the following annotated suggestions for further reading. Reflect on the glimpses given to see which classics you might like to "reclaim."

Augustine, St. *The Confessions of St. Augustine*. Trans. John K. Ryan. Garden City, N.Y.: Doubleday, Image Books, 1960.

> This classic autobiography presents a personal account of the search for truth and eventual conversion of one of the outstanding figures of western Christianity. It is a confession of Augustine's sin and error in the face of God's goodness and truth as well as a confident proclamation of the divine rest that awaits us at the end of our faith journey. As a spiritual journal of the first order, *The Confessions* offers the reader not only a penetrating look into Augustine's character and deeds but also a unique document for understanding the meaning of commitment in the spiritual life.

Ciszek, Walter, S.J., with Daniel L. Flaherty. *He Leadeth Me*. Garden City, N.Y.: Doubleday, 1973.

> This saintly Jesuit priest tells the inside story of his years of hard labor in the prison camps of Siberia where he had to live his commitment to Christ under tortuous circumstances. Through long years of isolation and suffering, stripped of physical and religious consolations, God led him to a new depth of trust and spiritual surrender.

Lewis, C.S. *Surprised by Joy: The Shape of My Early Life*. New York: Harcourt, Brace & World, A Harvest Book, 1955.

> How Lewis passed from atheism and a habit of disbelief to a sincere commitment to Christianity is a narrative of one man's pursuit of God and eventual joyful consent to grace. The experience of joy is integral to Lewis' conversion. In the end his religious experience is but a pointer to something other and beyond, to a divine, forming mystery in whom we live and move from the beginning.

Since becoming a Christian, the author admits being no longer prone to mistake a signpost for the journey's end.

Merton, Thomas. *The Sign of Jonas.* Garden City, N.Y.: Doubleday, Image Books, 1956.

In this journal of a young monk, Merton records day-to-day experiences and meditations, doubts and uncertainties, difficulties and joys as he approaches solemn vows and ordination. This record of commitment is not the story of one man only but of every person who struggles to effect the closest possible union with God. The book's message is not confined to the cloister but reaches out to embrace all Christians who sincerely seek the sign of Jonas—the sign of Christ's resurrection.

Muto, Susan Annette. *Meditation in Motion.* Garden City, N.Y.: Doubleday, Image Books, 1986.

This practical book encourages commitment to those seemingly chance encounters with God's forming grace that become over a lifetime avenues to faith deepening and meditative reflection. If we learn to recognize everyday moments as messengers of the transcendent, our inner lives will be transformed. The book suggests that no matter how busy we are, we can find time for spiritual refreshment and renewal.

Newman, Cardinal John Henry. *Apologia Pro Vita Sua.* Garden City, N.Y.: Doubleday, Image Books, 1956.

One of the great literary and spiritual classics of all time, Cardinal Newman's *Apologia* records the changes that took place in his religious opinions from his first childhood experiences until finally, after years of study and deliberation, all doubts resolved, "in perfect peace and contentment," he entered "the one Fold of Christ," the Catholic Church. This account of living commitment is unsurpassed in its sheer power of style, its remarkable absence of pose, its simple dignity. It reveals the intimate self of a sensitive and reserved man. Its meticulous care for accuracy of detail and the logical unfolding of events of grace traces the steps that led Newman from doubt to surrender.

Pope John XXIII. *Journal of a Soul*. Trans. Dorothy White. New York: McGraw-Hill, 1965.

This journal, of which Pope John says, "My soul is in these pages," was begun at age fourteen. One of Angelo Giuseppe Roncalli's early aspirations was to find a way of becoming like the saints. The diaries were continued almost without a break across sixty-seven years, the last entry being written about six months before his death in 1963. Humility and love were his constant strivings, obedience and peace his motto. His journal helps the reader to understand how the simple peasant boy achieved the greatness, the love of humanity, and the interior spiritual strength that invigorated his pontificate and inaugurated an era of reform and renewal within the church. It gives overwhelming testimony to the fruits of a life dedicated to spiritual perfection and to the belief that "God is everything."

PART 2

Commitment
and the
Threefold Path

ADVANCE PREPARATION
Before beginning this division of the formation guide, be sure that you have read Part Two, Chapters 4, 5, 6, and 7 of the original text.

GOAL

ON YOUR OWN
Read over the goal and consider its meaning for your own life.

IN YOUR GROUP
After opening with prayer, start the session with the facilitator reading, or asking someone else to read, the goal for this gathering.

GOAL
To describe the paths of obedience, poverty of spirit, and chaste love as directives for discipleship that all are to follow.

RETURN TO THE MESSAGE

ON YOUR OWN
Consider the following key words and phrases, relating their message to your own situation. Copy some of the related passages you spontaneously marked in the original text using the extra space provided. Add any key words and phrases not already on the list.

IN YOUR GROUP
As the facilitator guides this portion of your small group session, offer your thoughts on some of the words and phrases that were especially meaningful to you.

1. *The Threefold Path*

- The evangelical counsels of obedience, poverty of spirit, and chaste love are distinct directives for discipleship.
- This universal path of holiness, given by Jesus and upheld by the church, is not optional if we seek real growth in Christ; it is the underpinning of any Christian formation whatsoever.
- The way in which we, as committed Christians, express these graced directives points to the depth of our spiritual life; it points to our willingness to be formed in the image of God to which Jesus invites his disciples.

Your Thoughts:

2. Obedience

● Obedience, in the widest sense, entails the graced openness of people to listen to (Latin: ob-audire) the providential meaning of events in our lives.

● Obedience enhances our ability to attend to the forming presence of God in immediate situations and over a lifetime.

● The three components that interact to enable our growth in becoming good listeners are readiness, willingness, and respectful dialogue.

Your Thoughts:

_____

3. Readiness

● The openness asked of us by Jesus invites us to develop a readiness to surrender to anything that manifests itself as a possible disclosure of the divine direction of our life.

● The Spirit guides our discipleship in obedience to Christ's formative word addressing mind and heart.

● Our powers of obedience mature as we grow in commitment and meet the future with courage.

Your Thoughts:

4. *Willingness*

- Christian obedience is courageous because it is a sharing in the obedience of Jesus to the Father's will.
- Listening in faith calls for the willingness to say "Yes, Father" to what is divinely formative in our life and world.

Your Thoughts:

_____

5. *Respectful Dialogue*

- God's will comes to us in the form of appeals, invitations, and challenges, in concrete dialogue with the people and events that make up our day-to-day life.
- We must listen together to the many manifestations of the formation mystery in the world, for Christ is present in each of us in a unique way.
- Personal intimacy with Christ and the disclosure of divine directives in one another and in our own church, as our master-listener, constitute the essential components of obedience.

Your Thoughts:

6. Poverty of Spirit

• Poverty of spirit is a disposition of the heart that informs our approach to the natural and cultural things in and around us.

• It calls for the wise and respectful use not only of talents but also of outside things that takes into account their innermost form and considers how their use will affect others.

• Poverty as a path to holiness points also to the command to share what we have with the poor in a manner that remains responsive to the demands of social and economic justice.

Your Thoughts:

---

7. Possessiveness

• A major obstacle to poverty of spirit is our tendency, as fallen persons, to become so caught up in using and possessing objects and talents that we end up abusing them and others around us.

• If we become possessed by our possessions, all higher modes of presence to things are paralyzed; the pride form obscures our sense that all is gift.

Your Thoughts:

8. *Gifts from God*

● Nothing is more important in the quest for Christian maturation than to grow daily in an appreciation of the gifts of culture and nature.

● In poverty of spirit, objects, talents, knowledge, and sensitivities are appreciated as gifts from God.

● Care for and enjoyment of these gifts should be moderated by a recurrent movement to distance ourselves from them while tending to them.

Your Thoughts:

---

9. *Detachment or Daily Distancing*

● The Christian transformation of poverty into spiritual wealth begins with detachment; letting go of inordinate attachments frees us to see things reverently, in compatibility with their deepest form and meaning.

● Detachment prevents us from being tied permanently to things, from being fixated on only the surface dimension of their significance.

● Daily distancing permits us to go beyond the shell of things into the mystery they hide; we affirm the horizon against which things arise in their ultimate meaning as gifts and as pointers to the "more than."

Your Thoughts:

10. Poverty of Being

● Only by admitting our innate poverty, our vulnerability as humans, can we awaken to the grace of transcendence in Christ and thereby begin our journey toward Christian maturity.

● It is by acknowledging our utter dependency on God and surrendering to his compassion that we become able to carry out the singular mission we are called to live out in communion with others.

● To acknowledge our poverty is at the same time to reclaim our spiritual richness, for poverty is a symbolic pointer to our hunger and thirst for presence to the Most High.

Your Thoughts:

---

11. In the Light of Hope

● Hope is a disposition which teaches us that this world cannot offer us lasting peace, for nothing but God can fulfill the restless yearning of the human heart.

● In the light of hope, we are slowly loosened from the things on which our hopes may be glued; we begin to deal with things in a caring yet detached manner, as stewards not owners.

● We become able to enjoy and praise in thanksgiving the limited goodness, truth, and loveliness of the things of this world; we see them as a disclosure of the world awaiting us in times to come.

Your Thoughts:

12. Jesus' Way of Poverty

● Jesus asks us in the midst of our poverty to place our trust in the Father; he tells us that the Father's love and care will never be taken away from us.

● Jesus shows us in countless ways how the gifts of nature and culture should be used respectfully and lovingly in inner detachment and poverty of spirit.

● The attitude of Christ, which must become our own, is his kenotic love, his willingness to empty himself, not to cling to anything, to choose to become a servant.

Your Thoughts:

---

13. Chaste Love

● Our lives from their earliest days are an invitation to togetherness; committed love makes people friends and companions with one another on the road of maturation in the Lord.

● To become fully human and truly committed, love has to be "chastened" or "purified" of self-centered passions and purposes, anxious needs, and overdependent demands; only when love is chaste can we diminish the tendency to use and abuse ourselves as commodities for pleasure, as sources of need fulfillment or ego-enhancement.

● Chastened or purified love expresses the appreciative aspect of human love and is a commitment never to violate the God-given integrity, dignity, or unique unfolding of self and others.

● In humility, we acknowledge and affirm the limited yet loving persons we are called to become in the life situations allotted to us.

● To learn to live chastely and lovingly in the Spirit of Christ takes a lifetime; we must continually strive to affirm ourselves and confirm others because of the transforming love of Christ for each of us.

Your Thoughts:

14. *Healing Power of the Threefold Path*

- Healing, the road to wholeness and harmony, can be found in the threefold path laity are called to live in their own fashion.
- Obedience heals fragmentation and restores us to unity with the events of unfolding reality.
- Poverty of spirit enables us to transcend material goods as ultimate, to transform matter by revealing its spiritual meaning, to be aware of things as pointers to the mystery of all that is.
- Chaste love binds the break between individuals, cultures, races, creeds, and religions; it overcomes the dividing forces of disrespect and self-alienation that infect fallen human life.

Your Thoughts:

———————————————

Other Key Words and Phrases:

REFLECT UPON THE MEANING

ON YOUR OWN
Complete the following exercise. Where would you locate yourself between the two extremes for each of the following continuums? Put an X at the place representing you at this time in your spiritual life. Reflect on why you are at this point, and consider if this is an area in which you could benefit by being open to spiritual growth.

EXERCISE ON YOUR OWN:

1. └───┘

Am totally comfortable accepting the threefold path as a distinct directive for discipleship	Am totally uncomfortable accepting the threefold path as a distinct directive for discipleship

2. └───┘

See the counsel of obedience as something that sets me free	See the counsel of obedience as something that limits my freedom

3. └───┘

See poverty of spirit as totally realistic and applicable to my life today	See poverty of spirit as totally unrealistic and nonapplicable to my life today

4. |_____|

See myself and others   See myself
as companions on   and others as
on the road of   having totally
maturation in the   individualistic
Lord   relationships with
                                         the Lord

ON YOUR OWN
Reflect upon the following discussion statements and subsequent questions. Then write your responses in the space provided. To enhance your grasp of this aspect of self-direction, you may want to refer to the original text or the *Return to the Message* section of this guide.

IN YOUR GROUP
As the facilitator guides this portion of the session, try to offer some personal reflections on the questions.

DISCUSSION STATEMENTS AND QUESTION CLUSTERS FOR DEPTH:

1. **The authors identify the threefold path as a distinct directive for discipleship and the universal path of holiness.**

   a. What does it mean to you to be a disciple of Christ? Why is following the threefold path a helpful directive for living as his disciple?

b. In what way is this threefold path a "universal path of holiness"? Why universal? Why holiness?

c. In what ways are "being a disciple of Christ," "being on a universal path of holiness," and "becoming spiritually mature" related to one another?

d. As Christians, how do the three descriptions above relate to our "call to commitment"? In what way can following the threefold path help you answer your own unique call?

2. **At the end of the chapter on obedience, the authors suggest that committing ourselves to a life of obedience may at times prove to be counter-cultural.**

a. Why do you think they say that? Why do you think that obedience has a negative connotation for many people in our culture today? How do you personally react to God's directive for obedience? Are you comfortable or uncomfortable with it? Why do you think this is so?

b. How was Christ's life counter-cultural in his times? In what ways was obedience also an issue then? How did Christ demonstrate his obedience to his own call given by the Father? As a disciple of Christ, would you accept this willingly, or, like Peter, might you have tried to talk Christ out of being true to his call? Why do you believe Christ responded as he did to Peter in Matthew 16:23?

c. Think back over your life and consider whether you have ever been in a situation where being obedient to your unique life call resulted in your being counter-cultural. What was that situation? What did it feel like? How did you handle the situation?

3. **The authors tell us that obedience entails the openness to listen to the providential meaning of events in our lives and suggest that readiness, willingness, and respectful dialogue enable our growth in becoming good listeners to our call to commitment.**

a. Why do you think obedience entails openness and listening? What is it we are to be open to? What is it we are to be ready for? What is it we are to listen to? What is it we are to listen for? Who guides our discipleship in obedience?

b. What is it that obedience invites us to become? Why might that invitation be seen as an adventure in freedom rather than a limit to our freedom? How does obedience help us to make choices to be who we most deeply are and who we are intended to become as spiritually mature Christians?

c. What kind of willingness on our part does listening in faith call for? In what way is disobedience an act of the will? From what do people who disobey isolate themselves?

d. How and where does God's will come to us? What is it that we must dialogue with to learn God's will? Why do you imagine that some people wish for a "hot line to heaven" to know for sure?

4. **The authors define poverty of spirit as a disposition calling for the wise and respectful use of natural and cultural things.**

a. According to the authors, what is a major obstacle to poverty of spirit? How does this obstacle affect our use and possession of objects? How does it affect our use and possession of our talents? How does it sometimes affect the way in which we relate to others? What are the things our culture tends to make idols of? What, if any, are the "idols" in your own life?

b. How should we, in our quest for Christian maturation, view the things of culture and nature? How often, in a single day, do you behold things in that way? What are some of the things that you daily stop to appreciate as gifts from God?

c. What does it mean to detach ourselves from the surface meaning of things? What does "daily distancing" permit us to do? How does that affect our enjoyment of the objects, talents, and even the people around us? What are some of the things that you see as pointers to a wider horizon?

d. What does it mean to have "inordinate" or ultimate attachments? Consider thoughtfully what are the inordinate attachments or "little addictions" that you need to begin to let go of. What are they?

5. **The authors present another aspect of poverty of spirit as the basic poverty of being human that we all share, the reality of experiencing lives that are brief and passing.**

   a. As the authors explain it, what is the poverty of being human all about? What does it require that we admit and acknowledge? Why do you think making these acknowledgments and admissions is difficult for many people in our culture today?

   b. What do these admissions awaken in us? How is this related to beginning our journey toward Christian maturity?

   c. What are we able to reclaim because of these acknowledgments? To what is our poverty a symbolic pointer? In what does Jesus ask us to trust in the midst of our poverty? What examples of living in poverty of spirit does Christ provide for us?

   d. Do you agree or disagree with the authors when they say that hope teaches us that this world cannot offer us lasting peace? What does it mean to deal with things as a steward rather than as an owner? What are the things of this world that you are most able to enjoy and praise in thanksgiving?

6. **The authors explain that chastened or purified love expresses the appreciative aspect of human love; it makes people companions on the road of maturation in the Lord.**

   a. Of what must love be "chastened" or "purified" in order for us to become fully human and truly committed? How does this chastening express the appreciative aspect of human love? What is chastened love a commitment never to do? What is it a commitment to do in relation to self and others?

   b. What part does the disposition of humility play in our being able to chasten love? Teresa of Avila once said that humility is to walk in the truth of who we are. Reflect on what that statement means to you. What is its message for you personally?

   c. How did Christ teach that all are loved by him and hence worthy to be loved by one another? Describe what Christ-like committed love would look like in your own everyday life.

7. **The authors suggest that healing, the road to wholeness and harmony, can be found in the threefold path.**

   a. What is the fragmentation that obedience is capable of healing? What can it restore?

   b. What does poverty of spirit enable us to do that will bring healing?

   c. What are the kind of wounds that chaste love can bind up?

   d. Recall a time in your own life where following one or all of these counsels led to these kinds of healing. What was the situation? Which counsels were in evidence? Describe the healing that they brought.

RELATE TO SCRIPTURE

ON YOUR OWN

Read the scriptures from your Bible. Then write down your responses to the questions for each of the selections, using the context of the "commitment window" provided by this part of the guide.

IN YOUR GROUP

As the facilitator uses the focus passages and questions to guide the session, take the opportunity to express the spontaneous insights you have received. Be sure to have your Bibles with you so that you can refer to specific passages more easily.

SCRIPTURE STATEMENTS AND QUESTION CLUSTERS FOR BREADTH:

1. **The first set of scriptures will have us look at people in terms of their obedience to the providential meaning of events in their lives.**

    a. Read 1 Samuel 3:1–10. Obedience involves openness and listening. What we often have to realize first is that God is calling to us in our lives. This point is clearly made in the person of Samuel in the event related in this story.

        1) What concrete dialogue with Eli helped Samuel to know that it was God calling him? What are the necessary components for obedience that Samuel's response reveals?

        2) In what ways are we, like Samuel, unaware of when God may be speaking to us through the events of our lives?

b. Read 2 Kings 5:1–17. Naaman, a foreigner of the Syrian army, learned from the prophet Elisha that God asks for our obedience in the ordinary events rather than the extraordinary ways we sometimes seek.

1) What was Naaman asked to do? Why do you think he resisted being obedient in the manner in which Elisha requested? What concrete dialogue convinced him to do otherwise?

2) Reflect on your own life. Can you recall a time when you, too, resisted obedience to the ordinary? Why did you resist? What was the situation? What was the outcome?

c. Read Exodus 3:1–22; 4:1–17. The great leader Moses was initially reluctant to obey his unique life call.

1) What are the objections that Moses puts before God as to why he should not answer his call? (Note verses 3:11, 3:13, 4:1, and 4:10.) Why do you think Moses responded in this way? What about his call to commitment may have seemed risky? How did God reassure him? Why do you think Moses was obedient in the face of so many unknowns?

2) Reflect for a few moments on a time you may have hesitated in obeying your call when a glimpse of it was revealed through the everyday events of your life. What was the situation? Why did you hesitate?

d. Read Matthew 4:18–20 and Mark 1:16–20. The accounts of Christ calling Peter, Andrew, James and John are recorded in all three of the synoptic gospels.

1) How do they respond to Christ's call? Why do you imagine that they obediently followed immediately? What might they have seen in Christ that would have them say yes without question?

2) Can you recall a time you willingly said yes to an aspect of your unique call to commitment? What was the situation? What did you say yes to?

e. Read Luke 5:1–11. Luke's retelling of this event provides some additional insight.

1) What does it add to our knowledge of the event? As fisher-men who knew their profession, why do you think they obeyed Christ's invitation? How do you imagine them doing so—willingly in trust or skeptically in doubt?

2) Why did Peter respond as he did in verse 8? What had he realized through this event? What does this added insight suggest about why they followed Christ without question?

2. **The second set of scriptures consider poverty of spirit, the wise and respectful use of natural and cultural things.**

   a. Read Ecclesiastes 2:4–12, 24–25; 3:12–14; 12:13. As part of the wisdom literature, this book is often associated with Solomon. Whoever the person writing this essay, the above verses relate to poverty of spirit. How do they reveal the obstacle to poverty of spirit? Which verses tend toward overcoming this obstacle? Which components discussed by the authors do you see evidenced in those verses?

b. Read 1 Chronicles 29:10–20. In this prayer David illustrates a perhaps deeper level of spiritual maturity. After the materials for God's temple have been offered by himself and others, David speaks these words to the assembly. Which different components of poverty of spirit, as described by the authors, does David's prayer exemplify? What personal message for you do David's words hold?

c. Read Psalm 104. Psalms are the poetry most associated with David who composed and sang so many. This inspirational psalm of praise recognizes well the gifts from God, as well as humankind's poverty of being. As you reflect on this reading, consider all the different works of God that this writer acknowledges. For which of the things he mentions have you felt thankfulness to God? Note also verses 29 and 30. What aspect of poverty of being do they reveal?

d. Read Matthew 6:24–33 and Luke 12:22–31. In this teaching of Christ, found in both Matthew and Luke, the conditions for poverty of spirit are reassuringly presented. Of what are we reassured in these verses? What sage direction is given to us? What aspects of detachment brought out by the authors are found in these verses? In what way is this an easy or a difficult teaching for you personally?

3. **These last scriptures look at the chastened or purified love that signifies the appreciative aspect of human love.**

a. Read 1 Peter 4:8–11. This passage in Peter's letter has elements of chaste love and poverty of spirit. In verse 10, of what are we to be good stewards? What do the words in verse 8, "... love covers a multitude of sins," mean to you?

b. Read 1 Samuel 18:1–9; 19:1–7; 20:1–42. The friendship between Jonathan and David illustrates chaste love, as described by the authors. Compare Jonathan's chaste love for David with Saul's unchaste love. What are the passions that kept Saul from the appreciative aspect of human love?

c. Read 2 Samuel 1:17–27 and 9:1–11. In chapter 1, how does David's elegy for Saul and Jonathan, after they are lost in a Philistine battle, show David's capacity for chaste love? What attitude toward Saul, who had long sought his death, does David show? Can you recall a time when you were able to affirm yourself and confirm one who sought you harm because of the transforming love of Christ for each of us? Chapter 9 introduces the healing element of the threefold path. How do David's actions manifest that healing?

d. Read Genesis 45:1–15 and 50:15–21. The story of Joseph being sold by his brothers is well known. These two later events are perhaps less familiar but show well Joseph's chaste love and the healing power of the threefold path. How does Joseph confirm his brothers and affirm his own unique life call? How in Chapter 50 do his brothers reveal their inability to trust in chaste love? Why do you think Joseph broke into tears? Can you think of any events in your own life where forgiveness of past actions resulted in family healing? What was one that most affected you personally?

RECORD YOUR DIALOGUE

ON YOUR OWN

Record that which touches your life, that which inspires you and deepens your awareness of your life direction in the light of your commitment to your own specific Christian faith and formation tradition.

IN THE GROUP

If your group has decided to allot a short time for notebook sharing, you may, if you wish, offer insights that might benefit the other members of the group.

RECLAIM THE CLASSICS

ON YOUR OWN

Read over the following annotated suggestions for further reading. Reflect on the glimpse given to see if this may be a classic that you might like to "reclaim."

a Kempis, Thomas. *The Imitation of Christ.* Ed. Harold C. Gardiner. Garden City, N.Y.: Doubleday, Image Books, 1955.

   Written by a monk for monks, yet a springboard for all Christians concerned with the interior life, *The Imitation* is a series of meditations pointing the way by which one may follow the teachings and example of Christ's life. It offers timeless inspiration for pathfinders who seek the peace and confidence only God can offer.

de Caussade, Jean-Pierre. *Abandonment to Divine Providence.* Trans. John Beevers. Garden City, N.Y.: Doubleday, Image Books, 1975.

   In this classic guide to a life of obedience, poverty, and chastity, de Caussade outlines the means to attain holiness through total surrender to God and cooperation with God's will in one's everyday life situation. He emphasizes acceptance of the present moment as "an ever-flowing source of holiness." Such listening (*ob-audire*) is the central concern of the soul seeking God.

Kierkegaard, Søren. *Purity of Heart Is To Will One Thing: Spiritual Preparation for the Office of Confession.* Trans. Douglas V. Steere. New York: Harper & Row, Torchbooks, 1956.

   This edifying discourse is for men and women who seek to be drawn into water that is "70,000 fathoms deep," where life depends not upon half-measures but upon faith. Kierkegaard addresses "that solitary individual" who, instead of escaping into double-mindedness, chooses to come face to face in purity of heart with his or her destiny. Kierkegaard situates the individual before God, lending ultimate seriousness to the questions each must answer: Do I, or do I not, truthfully, sincerely, honestly will one thing? Do I revere the value of personal vocation? Do I depend ultimately upon faith?

Metz, Johannes Baptist. *Poverty of Spirit*. Trans. John Drury. Paramus, N.J.: Newman Press, 1968.

Assent to God starts when we can sincerely say *yes* to ourselves, to our innate lack of self-sufficiency. This total dependence on God, freely accepted, is what Metz calls poverty of spirit. Ordinary life with its gains and losses compels us, whether we like it or not, to drink the dregs of our poverty, while professing the mercy and generosity of God. Only when we live as Jesus did, acknowledging our humility and serving the poor, can we become truly rich.

Muto, Susan Annette. *Blessings That Make Us Be: A Formative Approach to Living the Beatitudes*. New York: Crossroad, 1984.

This book challenges the reader to personalize the threefold path of purgation, illumination, and union found in the beatitudes. These sayings of Jesus offer a solid foundation on which to build a life of faith. Paradox and promise, suffering and creativity, bondage and freedom—these and many more dynamics of formation comprise ''be-attitudes,'' attitudes of being that enable us to accept the challenges that come our way and to bless all who cross our path in compassion and care.

Teresa of Avila, St. *The Book of Her Life. The Collected Works of St. Teresa of Avila*, Volume One. Trans. Kieran Kavanaugh, O.C.D., and Otilio Rodriguez, O.C.D. Washington, D.C.: ICS Publications, 1976.

Resembling a long letter, Teresa's autobiography is a story of the mercy of God reaching out to the misery of a yearning soul. The saint is certain that all baptized Christians are called to the summit of the mount, to the innermost chambers of the castle, where the glory of God dwells. She describes with searing honesty how from an early age she began to receive God's abundant graces, but still resisted and refused to obey. While in the beginning she frustrated God's work, later she surrendered to ''his majesty'' wholly within her soul. Teresa's book is an extraordinary guide to living the path of obedience, poverty of spirit, and respectful love, ending in a resolve to seek perfection and walk always in the way of prayer.

van Kaam, Adrian. *The Vowed Life.* Denville, N.J.: Dimension Books, 1968.

In this most original book, the "threefold path" is traced from its anthropological and biological roots to its fruition in commitment and consecration to a Christian way of life lived in fidelity to one's vocation. The dynamics of the call and the healing power of the vows are developed alongside the obstacles to religious living in the western world. A superficial approach to involvement in our utilitarian culture contrasts with the author's emphasis on the implicit and explicit value of fully participating in the world as a spiritually committed person, in short, as one who listens to God, walks in the truth, and relates lovingly to all in need of care.

PART 3

Love and Commitment

ADVANCE PREPARATION
Before beginning this division of the formation guide, be sure that you have read Part Three, Chapters 8, 9, 10, 11, 12, and 13 of the original text.

GOAL

ON YOUR OWN
Read over the goal and consider its meaning for your own life.

IN YOUR GROUP
After opening with prayer, start the session with the facilitator reading, or asking someone else to read, the goal for this gathering.

GOAL
To consider mature love from the viewpoint of both marriage and singleness, understood as callings to follow Christ in communion with committed others.

RETURN TO THE MESSAGE

ON YOUR OWN
Consider the following key words and phrases, relating their message to your own situation. Copy some of the related passages you spontaneously marked in the original text, using the extra space provided. Add any key words and phrases not already on the list.

IN YOUR GROUP
As the facilitator guides this portion of your small group session, offer your thoughts on some of the words and phrases that were especially meaningful to you.

1.   Marital Intimacy and Commitment

• Christian marriage is a striking confirmation of the spiritual capacity of two people, once strangers to each other, to commit themselves to an intimate and lasting togetherness out of which a family emerges.

• The love and respect that Jesus taught to guide people's relationships is seen most particularly in marriage; growth in marital union and communion implies a twofold development of intimacy: love for oneself and devotion to one's spouse and children.

• Christ makes both husband and wife aware of the worst and best they can be for themselves and their families; he helps them see that a humble awareness of their limits must be complemented by a celebration of their gifts.

• In communion with Christ, spouses learn from experience how his word can become flesh in their daily marital celebration.

Your Thoughts:

2. Directives for Marriage

• Over the years, if a marriage is also a meeting place with God, spouses refine their radar, as it were, for what the Spirit may communicate through even the most common moments.

• The daily situations of work and play, laughter and tears, joy and pain, in which married people find themselves can disclose many hitherto unseen directives.

• Allowing the inspirations of the Spirit to become a guiding force in family life calls for stillness inwardly and simplicity outwardly.

• To set members free to find their own spiritual path, a family must be willing to transcend harsh, demanding styles of relating and develop instead a firm and gentle approach.

• Faithfulness to their commitments as married persons means that spouses vow to listen to what is going on in their daily life together and to let that input become the basis of honest dialogue.

Your Thoughts:

---

3. Reality of Marriage

• Being committed to the reality of marriage in and with Christ raises significantly one's chances of growing in mature love.

• True spirituality in marriage means partners are no longer victims of fads and choices out of tune with their commitments; it means facing the dreariness of everydayness in the light of the formation mystery.

• Fidelity to their commitment in family life means participating in the day-to-day unfolding of married life by confronting changing situations with care and courage; it means using each limit as an opportunity to confirm and renew one's own initial yes to this lasting life form.

• What supports such fidelity is the growing conviction that it is precisely within the marital life form that partners shall find their unique direction, their true selves hidden in God.

Your Thoughts:

4. Romantic Experience

● Our whole life is a yearning for participation in that which is "more than" we are; this longing, instilled by eternal love, impels us to find intimacy with a beloved, who represents the "more than" for us in some way.

● When we fall in love with someone, we may experience the temporary ecstasy of romantic affection; the gifted moment may remind us of the attraction of love divine.

● In romantic love, one has a kind of blindness to the limitations of the beloved; however, romantic rapture dims when the limitations of mere humanness combine with the sobriety of mundane, day-to-day existence.

● If we persist in the quest for romantic love alone, we may delay our chances for maturation, which implies a call to commitment arising from the depths of our heart.

● The fleeting intensity of romantic love, in and by itself, cannot promise lasting fulfillment; it may, however, awaken a person to a crucial awareness: that a lifelong dedication to a beloved spouse and family of one's own provides a way to share in God's own love for those to whom one is committed.

Your Thoughts:

---

5. Sacramental Commitment

● In the mysterious center of our life, the Spirit draws us to decide whether or not to establish a family of our own with this unique person.

● Sacramental marital love is a vow to serve lastingly each other's unique unfolding within the realistic boundaries of family and society; it is where two become one and share fully in the manifold joys and sorrows that life together brings them.

● This commitment of our whole being is never finished or perfect; still, the Holy Spirit grants to couples, living a solid marital commitment, the grace to transform sources of division and family tensions.

● Inspired by their commitment to one another before God, they are steadily disposed by grace to bind up wounds and heal differences, to seek again the restoration of harmony between them and their family.

Your Thoughts:

_____

6. *Dispositions of Committed Love*

● **Acceptance** guarantees on the part of the couple a permanent readiness to take one another as they are, in all the nuances of their personality revealed day after day, year after year.

● **Surrender** suggests a willingness to grow in spiritual maturity so that the gift each person is may bloom before the face of the Most High; it implies a readiness to alter gradually in oneself obstacles to mutual surrender.

● **Fidelity** in everyday life means that loving spouses will start to work without delay on their attitudes toward one another when their relationship is threatened; it diminishes absorption in other interests so that a couple can preserve tender attention to their own needs and those of their children.

● **Creative care** connotes a readiness to foster the vital, functional and social conditions that will facilitate the unique growth of each other.

Your Thoughts:

7.   Fallacies of Romantic Love

● A first fallacy of the cultural myth of the exclusive importance of romantic love is the suggestion that romantic pleasure represents the highest possible fulfillment of human life.

● Another is the fallacy that marital love would ideally be the continuation of only the romantic aspect of human love.

● A third fallacy is that there is a mysterious "only possible one" with whom alone we could establish a marital commitment.

● A lasting fallacy is the false notion that a marriage cannot be happy unless it is initiated by high-pitched romantic fascination.

Your Thoughts:

---

8.   Integration of Sexuality and Spirituality

● A major challenge in adult formation for Christian spouses is the integration of their sexuality and spirituality; the more comfortable spouses are in their sexual encounters, the more they may develop a true marital spirituality.

● Chaste, committed love means that married men and women wholeheartedly accept their sexuality as a precious gift of the Spirit, fostering the consonance of their life together.

● Respectful encounters in sexual intimacy reveal spouses to one another not only in their sexual potency and attractiveness, but also as unique manifestations of God's love within and around them.

● Spouses must take time to solve problems of disagreement and mutual misunderstanding by talking in an honest way about their divergent family backgrounds and feelings about sexual intimacy.

● Christian spouses can then live a committed life of unitive and procreative sexuality that remains in tune with their spirituality.

Your Thoughts:

9. *From Self-Centered to Other-Centered Love*

● Whatever our age, status, or state of life may be, we are called to love God above all else and to love others and ourselves in God.

● The lifelong maturation from self-centered love to other-centered love is difficult, demanding constant effort and attention; so entrenched are we in pride, in narcissistic needs, that to come to such a chastening of love is impossible without the grace of God.

● The height of growth in other-centered love is reached when we recognize ourselves and others as the imperfect creatures we are, while remaining utterly worthy of love in God's eyes.

● The dimension of celibate love, that should be lived by both single and married people, presupposes that one is centered in God who has loved us first; one then extends this love to others with attention and respect.

● The summit of the celibate component of mature Christian love is its unconditional willingness to celebrate the sacred uniqueness of others and to love them whether or not they can meet our needs.

Your Thoughts:

---

10. *Singleness as Consecration*

● Both Christian marriage and Christian singleness are forms of consecration in and through which the Lord himself is present in the church and in the world; both states share not only in the joy of resurrection but in the sadness of Christ's lonely passion.

● The single way of life, as a providential call, is one way to foster intimacy with Christ and to participate in the salvific history of humanity and culture.

● If Christian celibacy lived in the world by laity does not lead to the gift of oneself to Christ and others in joyful surrender, it can breed the conditions for self-centered preoccupation or mere sexual indulgence.

● Magnanimous love energizes single men and women to engage in labors congenial to them for which they are truly competent.

● Trying to make the best of their academic, scientific, artistic, technological, manual, administrative and religious gifts in myriad situations, in service of the spirit, is the single person's way of imitating Christ.

● In spiritual friendship, single persons respect one another's originality, strive to create a climate freed from tactics of seduction and manipulation, and, above all, foster a quality of encounter that opens them to the divine other in whom all have their being.

● Christian singles represent, in a special style and intensity, the receptivity every human being bears to the transcendent horizon of all that is.

Your Thoughts:

_____

Other Key Words and Phrases:

REFLECT UPON THE MEANING

ON YOUR OWN
Complete the following exercise. Where would you locate yourself between the two extremes for each of the following continuums? Put an X at the place representing you at this time in your spiritual life. Reflect on why you are at this point, and consider if this is an area in which you could benefit by being open to spiritual growth.

EXERCISE ON YOUR OWN:

1. |_____|

Able to see marriage as a
chosen response to
one's unique life
call to commitment
in Christ

Unable to see
marriage as a chosen
response to one's
unique life call to
commitment in
Christ

2. |_____|

See romantic love as
a possible prelude
to living one's
commitment to
marriage

See romantic
love as all
important in
living one's
commitment to
marriage

3. |_____|

Always able to
live a life of mature,
other-centered, Christian
love

Never able to
live a life of
mature,
other-centered,
Christian
love

4. └───┘

Always see singleness   Never see singleness
as a unique life   as a unique life
call to commitment   call to commitment

ON YOUR OWN
Reflect upon the following discussion statements and subsequent questions. Then write your responses in the space provided. To enhance your grasp of this aspect of self-direction, you may want to refer to the original text or the *Return to the Message* section of this guide.

IN YOUR GROUP
As the facilitator guides this portion of the session, try to offer some personal reflections on the questions.

DISCUSSION STATEMENTS AND QUESTION CLUSTERS FOR DEPTH:

1. **The authors suggest that, in Christian marriage, a man and a woman commit themselves to an intimate and lasting togetherness, to a faithful listening for God's directives in daily situations, and to the reality of a unitive and procreative marriage in Christ.**

   a. What does intimacy mean to you? Is it a word with which you are comfortable or uncomfortable? How does it pertain to one's inmost being? What is the twofold development of intimacy taught by Jesus that the authors suggest guides growth in marital union and communion? What part do awareness of limits and celebration of gifts play in intimacy?

b. What does it mean to you to grow in marital union and communion? What does being in communion with Christ mean to you? In what way can communion in Christ draw a couple closer together?

c. How do you and your family respond to life's daily situations such as work and play, laughter and tears, joy and pain? How might these serve as directives through which the Spirit may communicate? What is called for if we are to allow the inspirations of the Spirit to become a guiding force in our family life? What is needed to set family members free on their spiritual path? Consider how your own family relates. What is the balance between gentleness and firmness?

d. What does the word vow mean to you? Why do people today seem to find it so difficult to keep their marital vows? What does it mean if spouses vow to listen to what is going on in their daily life together? What would they be listening to? What part do honest dialogue and open communication play in a committed marriage?

e. If one is committed to the reality of marriage in and with Christ, to what is one committed? How is that a sign of mature love? Why does it take courage to live in fidelity to one's commitment in family life? What makes such fidelity to everydayness possible?

2. **The authors suggest that romantic love may serve for some as a prelude to committed love. They also identify some of the fallacies of romantic love.**

a. According to the authors, for what do we all long? In terms of your own experience, how do you know this to be true? What is the source of this longing? In what way does romantic love answer this yearning? Why is this fleeting rather than lasting?

b. Think of situations where you have seen people falling again and again into the trap of romantic love. What happens if we persist in the quest for romantic love alone? What causes romantic rapture to dim? How can the romantic experience serve to deepen our Christian spiritual life?

c.   What are the fallacies of romantic love that the authors present? How does our culture tend to support belief in these fallacies? Which of these fallacies have you believed in at one time or another in your life? What was the situation when you believed that fallacy? What happened that led to your personally recognizing this belief as fallacious?

3.   **The authors tell us that sacramental love is a vow to serve lastingly each other's unique unfolding within the realistic boundaries of family and society. They also present the dispositions of committed love that can facilitate this.**

a.   What does the word sacramental mean to you? How is it related to having something become sacred? What are events that you consider sacramental? What events are celebrated as sacraments within your faith tradition? Which of those do you hold sacred? How do you evidence that in your everyday life?

b.   How can a couple serve one another's unique unfolding in Christ and still become one? Why do you think that such a commitment of our whole being is never finished or perfect? How is that commitment elevated to a level of consecration? What assistance are we given to grow in this area? Who gives that assistance? How does all of this relate to our becoming spiritually mature?

c. Which one of the four dispositions of committed love is most like unconditional love? Why do we all want to be loved in that way? When have you most experienced that kind of love?

d. Why is surrender almost a counter-cultural disposition today? What does it mean to bloom where you are planted?

e. How does fidelity help to diminish our absorption in other interests that take us away from the care of our family? Why must fidelity involve the willingness to seek psychotherapy, marriage counseling, or spiritual direction, if this is really the only course of action, when a couple's relationship is seriously threatened? Based on your personal experience, is this an easy or difficult step for most couples? What makes it easy or difficult?

f. How do the authors define creative care? What does it mean to you to care? What does it mean to care creatively? What specific examples of provisions for health maintenance, recreational needs, social well-being, and spiritual development can you give from your own life? How do these demonstrate "creative" care to you?

4. **The authors suggest that the more comfortable spouses are in their sexual encounters, the more they may develop a true marital spirituality.**

   a. Why is this integration a major challenge in adult formation for Christian spouses? In what ways do current cultural preoccupations and the impact of the media add to that challenge?

   b. How do the deformative ideas and feelings about sex that one brings into a marriage influence a couple's growing toward an integrated, joyful sexuality in marriage? What must spouses do to solve the problems these deformative ideas and feelings cause?

   c. What is chaste, committed love as defined by the authors? What does chaste, committed love foster in a marriage? Why is the integration of sexuality and spirituality important for living a committed marital life?

5. **The authors say that the summit of other-centered love is its unconditional willingness to celebrate the sacred uniqueness of others and to love them whether or not they can meet our needs.**

   a. Why is the lifelong maturation from self-centered to other-centered love so difficult? In which relationships do you personally find it most difficult? How do you see our current culture adding to this difficulty? What do the authors mean when they talk about our pride form? What part does it play in our ability to grow toward mature love?

b. What do the authors say is the height of other-centered love? With whom are you most able to experience that kind of love? From whom have you experienced receiving mature love?

c. How do the authors define celibate love? What is the presupposition in which this kind of love is rooted? Why is this foundation necessary? What would celebrating someone's sacred uniqueness look like? Why is it so critical to love others whether or not they can meet our needs? In what ways do you feel our culture makes this difficult?

d. Why is our approach to love often one of "I'll love you, if you love me"? Recall a time when you did not approach loving in that way. What was the situation? What made it possible for you to love? Why is it considered mature Christian love to accept the risk that one may be asked to give love to others without receiving like love in return?

6. **The authors believe that both Christian marriage and Christian singleness are forms of consecration in and through which the Lord himself is present in the church and in the world.**

   a. In what way do both states share in the joy of resurrection and the sadness of Christ's lonely passion? How is the joy of Christ's resurrection a part of singleness as well as marriage? Why is loneliness a part of marriage as well as the single life call?

   b. What fallacies exist about the single life call in our culture? In what ways does our culture idealize and yet diminish the single life call? Why does our culture cause single persons to question their calling, to silence the whispers of the Spirit?

c. How is singleness a form of consecration? What makes it possible for singles to elevate their call to commitment to a call to consecration? Why is it important to have this vision of one's call? In what ways do single persons, in service of the Spirit, try to imitate Christ? How does singleness, as a symbol, express the solitary fullness of intimacy with the Trinity?

d. What are the aspects of other-centered love that may be present for single persons in spiritual friendships? How is such befriending a risk? In what way does a capacity for togetherness emerge out of aloneness with God?

RELATE TO SCRIPTURE

ON YOUR OWN
Read the scriptures from your Bible. Then write down your responses to the questions for each of the selections, using the context of the "commitment window" provided by this part of the guide.

IN YOUR GROUP
As the facilitator uses the focus passages and questions to guide the session, take the opportunity to express the spontaneous insights you have received. Be sure to have your Bibles with you so that you can refer to specific passages more easily.

SCRIPTURE STATEMENTS AND QUESTION CLUSTERS FOR BREADTH:

1. **The authors tell us that the love and respect Jesus taught to guide people's relationships is seen most particularly in marriage and that growth in marital union and communion implies a twofold development of intimacy.**

   a.   Read Matthew 22:36–40; Deuteronomy 5:1–22; 6:5–7. In verse 40 of Matthew, Jesus says that the whole law of Moses and of the prophets depends on these two commandments. What are they? Review Deuteronomy 5:1–22 (or Exodus 20:1–17). In what way do all of these depend on the two commandments that Jesus gave? Which relate to our relationship with God, which to our relationship with others? Reflect on Matthew 22:39. To which of your relationships do you most often envision this commandment applying? Why do the authors suggest that this love and respect is to be seen most particularly in marriage?

b. Read Mark 12:28–34 and John 13:34–35. Using Mark's retelling of the event, reflect again upon the commandments of which there are none greater. In what way are we to make the reign of God real in our life? In what way is our love of self dependent on our relationship with God? How is our love of others dependent on our relationship with God and self? Why do the authors suggest that growth in marital union and communion implies a twofold development of intimacy? In John 13, what qualifier does Jesus add to the command of loving others? What might living in this way give evidence of?

c. Read John 14:15–29 and John 15:1–17. In verses 14:15, 14:21, 14:23, and 15:10, what does Christ say that observing his commandments of love will show? What are we promised in verses 14:16–17 and 15:26? What are we given in verses 14:27 and 15:11? In what way do you experience these gifts personally in your life? After reflecting on these powerful passages of John's gospel, consider how being committed to the reality of marriage in and with Christ raises significantly one's chances of growing in mature love? In what way is marriage meant to be a meeting place with God?

d. Read 1 Corinthians 13:1–13. Paul describes love to the people of Corinth. In verses 1 to 3, how are we described as being if we lack love? How is love described in verses 4 to 6? In what situations and from whom have you experienced love as described here? In what situations and to whom have you extended this kind of love? How do these words make us aware of the best, and, by contrast, the worst, spouses can be for themselves and for their families?

2. **The authors suggest that romantic love, although perhaps a gifted, intense moment that temporarily reminds us of the attraction of love divine, cannot promise lasting fulfillment. It, along with the fallacies that exist concerning it, is not to be confused with committed mature love that arises from the depths of our heart.**

a. Read 2 Samuel 11:1–27; 12:1–26; Psalm 51. In verse 11:14, we see how David, struck by Bathsheba's beauty, experiences a "romantic" attraction for her. To what does David's attraction lead? In what ways is this similar to the "romance" aspect of love prevalent in our society today? What are the consequences and subsequent actions that follow David's encounter? In what way are these actions related to the "blindness" aspect of romantic love? In chapter 12, whom does the Lord use to open David's eyes? Consider verse 12:13. How does David respond to this insight? Psalm 51 is considered by many to be the one that David composed and sang to God following this event in his life. Reflect on verses 51:12–14. Think back to Part 1 when you looked at David's anointing. What two things are mentioned again in these verses? Prophecy revealed to David that this first son would die in childbirth. In verses 12:20–23, what does David say and do in response to the news? What in verse 12:24 suggests that David is beginning to mature in his love for Bathsheba? How is that deepening love blessed?

b. Read 1 Kings 1:11–37. How does this incident show David's devotion to Bathsheba and his son Solomon? Review the points the authors make concerning sacramental commitment. What elements of it can you see in this event?

c. Read 1 Kings 11:1–8. Solomon was blessed by God with great wisdom, yet his seeking after the "romantic experience" with foreign wives resulted in his losing what? How does this help show that the commitment of our whole being to God, self, and others is never finished or perfect? Why is it important not to turn one's heart from God?

d. Read 2 Samuel 13:1–21. How is Amnon "moved" by the romantic experience? What does he do in order to have that experience of "falling in love" realized? How is selfishness rather than the dispositions of committed love revealed by his actions? What feelings does he experience after the blindness of romantic love is lifted? What action does he take? What level of spiritual maturity does Amnon show in this response and action? In what ways do you see this lack of commitment or spiritual maturity in our culture today?

3. **The authors suggest that sacramental marital love is a vow to serve lastingly each other's unique unfolding, that it is where two become one inspired by their commitment to one another before God. They suggest also that the dispositions of such committed love include acceptance, surrender, fidelity, and creative care.**

   a. Read Isaiah 61:10; 62:1–5; Hosea 2:19–23. How do the prophets describe the relationship between God and Jerusalem in these passages? Why do you think they describe it in this way? What do the verses suggest to you about how God views the union of marriage? Which dispositions of committed love are expressed?

   b. Read John 3:27–29; Revelation 19:5–10; 21:1–7, 9. How does John the Baptist refer to Christ in John's gospel? Who is Christ's bride in Revelation 19:7–8? What does it mean in verse 19:9 to be invited to the wedding feast of the Lamb? What does this imagery suggest about the significance of marital vows? Which dispositions of committed love are expressed?

c. Read Genesis 2:24; Matthew 19:4–5; Mark 10:5–9; 1 Corinthians 6:12–17, 19. Reflect on what these verses are saying. What does it mean to you when "two become one"? How is it an intimate and lasting togetherness? In 1 Corinthians 6:15, with whom does it tell us we are one? In verse 6:17, what are we told happens when we are joined or "wedded" to the Lord? Who alone can satisfy the sense of "belongingness" for which we all yearn?

d. Read Ephesians 5:21–33; 6:1–4. Reflect on what Paul writes in this letter. In verse 5:25, what does it say a husband's love for his wife is to be like? Which counsel of the threefold path is this most like? In verse 5:22, what does it say a wife's relationship with her husband should be like? Which counsel of the three-fold path is this most like? Read verse 5:21 again. What are both spouses called to? What reason is given as to why? Read verse 5:33 again. What are both spouses called to? Of what relationship do verses 6:1–4 speak? What promise accompanies this command? What dispositions of committed love are expressed in these passages?

e. Read 1 Peter 3:1–7 and Proverbs 31:10–31. In what way does Peter's letter echo the one written by Paul? Wherein resides a woman's beauty? How is she described in Proverbs 31:25–26? Which dispositions of committed love are seen in these two passages?

4. **The authors suggest that the lifelong maturation from self-centered love to other-centered love is difficult. The height of growth in other-centered love is reached when we recognize ourselves and others as the imperfect creatures we are, while remaining utterly worthy of love in God's eyes.**

   a. Read Matthew 1:18–25; 2:13–15, 19–23; Luke 2:1–52. In Part 2, we saw the other-centered love of Ruth and Boaz. Now we reflect upon the other-centered love in the union of Mary and Joseph. How do these passages show Joseph's commitment to his own unique call from all eternity and the other-centered mature aspect of his love for Mary and Jesus?

   b. Read 1 Peter 3:8–18. After speaking about spouses in verses 3:1–7, the writer of Peter's letter goes on to describe the other-centered kind of love to which we are called. Which of the dispositions of committed love suggested by the authors are present in these words? In verse 11, what are we told to seek? What must we always be ready to do as explained in verse 15? In what manner are we to do this?

c. Read 1 John 4:1–24. This eloquent letter of John's contains some of the most beautiful images in holy scripture concerning love. Ponder this passage deeply. Of what are we first assured in verses 1 and 2? In verse 11, what are we told is the message that we have heard from the beginning? How does verse 16 explain that we came to know love? What do the words in verse 18 mean to you? What does it look like in your life "to love not in word or speech but in deed and truth"?

5. **The authors help us to see the other-centered aspect of mature love that can be manifested in the spiritual friendship of single persons also, for they represent, in a special style and intensity, the receptivity every human bears to the transcendent horizon of all that is.**

a. Read 2 Kings 2:1–14. This story of the friendship between the prophets Elijah and Elisha is a notable one. Consider Elisha's response in verses 2, 4, and 6. What aspect of love does this show? Recall an experience of your own where you experienced the beauty of such committed love. What was the situation? What were your feelings in that situation?

b. Read John 11:1–44. Nowhere is chaste love expressed more beautifully than in the life of Jesus. He is the model for all single persons in their relationships with others, and his love for his friends Lazarus, Mary and Martha is exemplary. Reflect on verses 5, 33, and 35 in this regard. Verse 35 is the shortest in all of holy scripture and yet its words are profound. What dispositions of committed love do these verses reveal? Recall a time in your own life when you experienced the kind of spiritual friendship and mature love that is illustrated here? What was the situation? In what way was your spiritual friendship manifested?

    c.   Read Luke 10:38–42 and John 20:11–18. What does Luke's gospel reveal about the spiritual friendship Jesus had for Mary and Martha? How does he show the aspect of other-centered love wherein we are to celebrate the sacred uniqueness of others whether or not they can meet our needs? What does John's gospel reveal about the spiritual friendship of Jesus with Mary Magdalene?

    d.   Read 1 Timothy 1:1–20; 3:14; 6:11–20; 2 Timothy 1:13–14. In Paul's letter to Timothy we again see a friendship rooted in faith. Consider verses 1:2, 1:18, and 6:11 in 1 Timothy. How does Paul address Timothy? What wise counsel does Paul share with his friend? Reflect on verses 1:13–14 in 2 Timothy. How are these words sage counsel for your own life? What else about Paul's message to Timothy is meaningful for your living mature, committed Christian love?

RECORD YOUR DIALOGUE

ON YOUR OWN
Record that which touches your life, that which inspires you and deepens your awareness of your life direction in the light of your commitment to your own specific Christian faith and formation tradition.

IN THE GROUP
If your group has decided to allot a short time for notebook sharing, you may, if you wish, offer insights that might benefit the other members of the group.

RECLAIM THE CLASSICS

Read over the following annotated suggestions for further reading. Reflect on the glimpses given to see which classics you might like to "reclaim."

Aelred of Rievaulx. *On Spiritual Friendship*. Trans. Mary Eugenia Laker. Washington, D.C.: Cistercian Publications, 1974.

Aelred advocated friendship on both the natural and the supernatural plane. Frankness, not flattery, generosity, not gain, patience in correction and constancy in affection are the marks of a true friendship. If a friend prays for another, the friendship will be extended to include Christ. "Thus ascending from that holy love with which he embraces a friend to that with which he embraces Christ, he will joyfully partake in abundance of the spiritual fruit of friendship, awaiting the fullness of all things in the life to come." According to Aelred, there is nothing more advantageous to human relationships than divinely inspired friendship. From being a friend to others, we become a friend of God; from being God's friend, we learn to befriend God's people.

Lewis, C.S. *The Four Loves*. London: William Collins, Fontana Books, 1963.

Though other authors from Ovid to St. Bernard, from St. Paul to Stendhal, have examined Affection, Friendship, Eros, and Charity, few have seen as well as Lewis how each merges into the other, how we can even become one with another person, as in marriage, without losing sight of the necessary and real difference between us. The author knows the peculiar values of each of these four loves without supposing any one of them to be all in all. He discerns as well the deceptions and distortions which can sever the first three from the divine love that must be the sum and goal of all. This anatomy of love is further illuminated by the author's gifts of immediacy, lucidity, and aptness of expression and illustration.

Lindbergh, Anne Morrow. *Gift from the Sea*. New York: Random House, A Vintage Book, 1965.

The setting of this highly acclaimed book is the seashore; the time, a brief vacation which lifted the author from the distractions of everyday existence into the sphere of meditation. As the sea tosses up its gifts—shells rare and perfect—so the mind, left to its ponderings, brings up its own treasures of the deep. The shells (channelled whelk, double-sunrise, argonauta) become symbols for the aspect of life this active woman is contemplating: the restlessness, pressures, and demands we face today; the hunger for leisure and silence; the call for inner peace and integration; the commitment to lasting, faith-filled relationships.

Muto, Susan Annette. *Celebrating the Single Life: A Spirituality for Single Persons in Today's World*. New York: Crossroad, 1989.

This book offers a compelling view of love and commitment that reflects the author's own call to the single vocation as a way of loving, as a wellspring for spiritual maturity. She does not promise that single persons who live in Christ will never feel loneliness, pain, or frustration, but she does hold out the vision that a spiritually grounded single life will lead to intimacy with God and inclusive care for others.

O'Connor, Flannery. *The Habit of Being: Letters of Flannery O'Connor*. Ed. Sally Fitzgerald. New York: Farrar, Straus, & Giroux, 1979.

This collection contains a simple yet immensely significant testimony to the underlying meaning of O'Connor's life and work as a novelist and short-story writer. With a sometimes humorous, sometimes intense, but always penetrating style, Flannery restores dignity and value to the calling to a single life. She reveals in her work how grace can use human limits to reveal the heights of love.

Vanauken, Sheldon. *A Severe Mercy*. New York: Harper & Row, Publishers, 1977.

This is a remarkable story of young love and marriage as told by the husband of Davy, whose death, while devastating him, also becomes an opening to new life and an affirmation of their mutual conversion to Christianity, thanks to the support and friendship of C.S. Lewis. This reminiscence evolves into a stunning and beautiful story of marital love that both shatters and heals.

William of St. Thierry. *On Contemplating God.* Trans. Sister Penelope. Spencer, Mass.: Cistercian Publications, 1971.

Friend and contemporary of St. Bernard, William is a poet of love who takes into account the practical ups and downs of monastic and Christian life. While setting forth the principles that lead the soul to the plenitude of love, he realistically cites the obstacles along the way. In the end, William establishes that happiness consists of contemplating God, of seeing the Holy face to face in an eternal embrace of love and allegiance.

PART 4

Living Community

ADVANCE PREPARATION
Before beginning this division of the formation guide, be sure that you have read Part Four, Chapters 14 and 15 of the original text.

GOAL

ON YOUR OWN
Read over the goal and consider its meaning for your own life.

IN YOUR GROUP
After opening with prayer, start the session with the facilitator reading, or asking someone else to read, the goal for this gathering

GOAL
To explore the signs of a sound Christian community of committed laity and to distinguish the Spirit-inspired, graced ground from which such a gathering emerges.

RETURN TO THE MESSAGE

ON YOUR OWN
Consider the following key words and phrases, relating their message to your own situation. Copy some of the related passages you spontaneously marked in the original text using the extra space provided. Add any key words and phrases not already on the list.

IN YOUR GROUP
As the facilitator guides this portion of your small group session, offer your thoughts on some of the words and phrases that were especially meaningful to you.

---

1. Crowd

- A crowd is a group bound together by a temporary uplift caused by contagious excitement about a time-bound cause.
- Different from transient enthusiasm is inner growth over a long period of time by means of committed togetherness, supported by attentiveness to the deeper meanings of life.

Your Thoughts:

---

2. Collectivity

- A well organized collectivity is a diverse group that works "all for one and one for all."
- A collectivity is a group that demands allegiance and uniformity in regard to its own special expressions and practices, rather than beginning with and respecting where people are in their God-given uniqueness.

● Too often Christians confuse community with a collective rigidity that molds rather than forms, that imposes rather than frees.

Your Thoughts:

---

3. *Formation Community*

● A formation community consists of a group of committed Christians in search of spiritual maturity.

● Community members seek to deepen prayer in common ways offered by the church and to increase their love for God and their willingness to listen to the invitations of grace in the circumstances and events in their everyday lives.

● The chief signs of a sound Christian community of committed laity include five C's—congeniality, compatibility, compassion, courage, and competence.

Your Thoughts:

---

4. *Congeniality*

● Congeniality means to be at home with the mystery of our being created in the form and likeness of God.

● Lay Christians come together in a Christian community with the aim of confirming each one's personal commitment to Christ and respecting each one's unique calling.

Your Thoughts:

5. *Compatibility*

- Compatibility means to undergo with others the limits of a situation; to endure patiently the frame of reference in which one finds oneself by virtue of one's calling.
- Lay people's particular way of life in the world, while being congenial to their integral calling in Christ, must be compatible, insofar as possible, with the everyday sensitivities of those around them.

Your Thoughts:

---

6. *Compassion*

- Compassion means to suffer empathically with our own and others' vulnerability.
- The more we come to know one another with our failings and vulnerabilities, the more we realize how profound our need is for understanding and forgiveness.
- Compassion is the glue that binds a group together, for it teaches us to bear with and love one another.
- Such love is only possible through Christ who elevated the ideal of humanity to a new height by making compassion one of its central aspirations.

Your Thoughts:

7. Courage

- Courage prompts commitment of the heart to persevere in the formation of Christian community, whatever the cost.
- Certain lay communities and associations survive because they have the courage to persist in the essentials of their founding vision and the courage to be open to changing times.

Your Thoughts:

---

8. Competence

- The communal disposition of competence implies that each member strives to excel in the gifts and talents he or she has been given.
- The pursuit of competence and professional excellence grows out of a life of commitment; it fosters maturation, enhances functionality, and in no way detracts from productivity and true spirituality.

Your Thoughts:

---

9. Humanistic Community

- A humanistic community is explainable in terms of human inventiveness and the sciences that expound and sustain it.
- Excellent as it may be, a humanistic community cannot satisfy the deepest longings of the heart.
- We need to go beyond humanistic efforts without neglecting their compatible insights; we need to recognize that inspired aspirations transcend all that group dynamics, sensitivity training, encounter techniques, and the psychology of human relationships can teach us.

Your Thoughts:

10. Pneumatic Community

● Only a community of Christian formation that relies also on the power of the Holy Spirit can become a "pneumatic" community, as distinguished from a merely "humanistic" community.

● The pneumatic community nourishes us spiritually before we know mentally what is going on in our graced togetherness.

● A true community of Christian formation takes us up into a wider divine community beyond our boldest dreams, the community of the mystical body of Christ.

● No human effort can pretend to build this body; we can only express awe and gratefulness for the ecclesial communion in which we already live as companions in faith.

Your Thoughts:

---

11. Spirit-Inspired Capacity

● A mark of Christian community is the Spirit-inspired capacity to surpass personality differences and to overcome human antipathies; it is to remain committed even when difficulties arise.

● Christian community members try, in the light of their baptism, strengthened by the Holy Spirit and by church teachings and traditions, to purify and transcend the natural obstacles any human community has to face.

● Instead of striving to outdo one another in competitive efforts, Christians are called to complement one another by their different contributions to the well-being of the community.

● People in a pneumatic community expect that the Holy Spirit will help members contribute to the common good; they are ready to celebrate together in loving appreciation a wide diversity of gifts.

Your Thoughts:

12. Affinity of Grace

• What binds members of a Christian community together is not a mere human affinity but an affinity of grace.

• First, as lay Christians gathered in the name of the Lord, we strive to appreciate not only our differences but also our hidden likeness in the mystery of transforming love.

• A second aspect of our graced affinity as community members resides in our complementarity in the Spirit; each of us is called to be a unique Christ-form while serving the common good in a firm yet gentle way.

• A third outflow of our faith in the affinity of grace is a shared openness to the inspiration of the Spirit directing us toward the particular aims and goals God wants us to achieve in the body of Christ.

• Because each graced grouping is a special expression of the body of Christ, Christians grow together in likeness to what they share most deeply: membership in God's family by adoption.

Your Thoughts:

---

13. Moments of Renewed Inspiration

• A community can lose its awareness of mystery and ministry and be reduced to a kind of service organization.

• Leaving no room for abiding in the Spirit, attunement to pneumatic inspiration begins to erode; we risk becoming alienated from the holy ground that nurtures our pneumatic community's purpose of existence.

• Soon the community started with such hope begins to crumble as members sink into a kind of low-grade communal depression.

● Paradoxically, the Holy Spirit may use such a moment of crisis to reawaken the members to the central importance of prayer and the priority of restoring time and again, with God's grace, their initial inspiration.

Your Thoughts:

_____

Other Key Words and Phrases:

REFLECT UPON THE MEANING

ON YOUR OWN

Complete the following exercise. Where would you locate yourself between the two extremes for each of the following continuums? Put an X at the place representing you at this time in your spiritual life. Reflect on why you are at this point, and consider if this is an area in which you could benefit by being open to spiritual growth.

EXERCISE ON YOUR OWN:

1. |_____|

See a crowd,   See a crowd,
collectivity, and   collectivity, and
formation community   formation
as totally different   community as
                                                  totally the same

2. |_____|

Totally able to see   Totally unable to
the five C's as signs of   see the five C's
a sound Christian   as signs of a
community of committed   sound Christian
laity   community of
                                                  committed laity

3. |_____|

See a humanistic   See a
community and   humanistic
a pneumatic community   community and
as totally different   a pneumatic
                                                  community as
                                                  totally the same

4. |_____|

Able to see   Not able to see
that what binds   that what binds
us together as a   us together as a
Christian community   Christian
is an affinity of grace   community is an
                                      affinity of grace

ON YOUR OWN
Reflect upon the following discussion statements and subsequent questions. Then write your responses in the space provided. To enhance your grasp of this aspect of self-direction, you may want to refer to the original text or the *Return to the Message* section of this guide.

IN YOUR GROUP
As the facilitator guides this portion of the session, try to offer some personal reflections on the questions.

DISCUSSION STATEMENTS AND QUESTION CLUSTERS FOR DEPTH:

1. **The authors begin Part 4 by distinguishing between a crowd, a collectivity, and a community.**

    a. What distinguishing factors of a crowd do the authors present? Picture yourself in a crowd of people gathered in Times Square on New Year's Eve or among the people lining the streets for the Rose Bowl Parade. What are some gatherings you have been in that were "crowd" situations like these? What was going on in and around you? What was your feeling toward the others present?

b. What distinguishing factors of a collectivity do the authors present? Picture yourself, or someone you love, entering basic training camp in a branch of military service or beginning first grade. What are some gatherings you have been in that were "collectivity" situations like these? What are the constructive aspects of a collectivity? What are the potential deformative aspects? How do you maintain your own unique call to commitment in a collectivity?

c. What characterizes a Christian formation community, as presented by the authors? Why do you think many people long to be embraced by a caring community? What distinguishes a strictly "needy" community from one where Christians seek a more mature life in Christ?

2. **The authors offer five C's as signs of a sound Christian formation community: congeniality, compatibility, compassion, courage, and competence.**

a. How do the authors define congeniality? What do lay Christians who come together confirm in each other? What might be signs that this first "C" was being violated in a formation community? In what way is respect basic to the congeniality factor?

b. How do the authors define compatibility? What is the relation-ship between congeniality and compatibility, between one's unique call to commitment and the limits of one's situation? What are directives that may be seen as incompatible? In what way is freedom basic to the compatibility factor?

c. How do the authors define compassion? Why does compassion become increasingly needed the more we come to know one another and the longer we meet together? What are we more able to know about ourselves and others as relationships deepen? Why does this help us realize how profound is our need for understanding and forgiveness? Why is this kind of love possible only through Jesus?

d. Why is courage described as a "commitment of the heart" to persevere? Why does perseverance take courage? What is the relationship of courage to the other C's? What are the two aspects of courage that may account for why some lay commu-nities and associations survive? What would be the result if one attempted to change quickly and completely the structure of an existing community?

e. What is implied by the communal disposition of competence? What is the relationship between the spiritual life and everyday competence? Why is it important that mature Christian communities overcome this split?

3. **The authors distinguish between a merely humanistic community and a pneumatic community.**

   a. What characterizes a humanistic community? What has been your experience with humanistic groups and some of the techniques used in them? What about them has been helpful? What of their limitations have you seen or experienced? Why do techniques alone perhaps not remedy one's inability to communicate with others? Why do the authors suggest that a humanistic community cannot satisfy the deepest longings of the heart?

   b. What distinguishes a pneumatic community from a merely humanistic one? What is the difference between mental nourishment and spiritual nourishment? What does it mean to you personally to know that you are a member of the body of Christ? Why is it that no human effort can pretend to build this body?

c. What is a "Spirit-inspired" capacity as distinct from a human effort alone? How are the usual obstacles any human community has to face overcome? Reflect again upon each of the five C's, and consider what part each of them plays in overcoming obstacles.

d. What is an affinity of grace versus a mere human affinity? What different aspects of this graced affinity as community members do the authors present? What is it that we most deeply share that unites us?

e. Because we never arrive, but are always on the way to Christian maturity, communities can lose their focus. What happens when a Christian formation community is reduced to a kind of service organization? Although Christian service is important, what do the authors suggest can be missing in a group that becomes just a service organization? Describe any experiences you may have had in such a service organization. What did you personally experience as missing?

f. What do you envision a low-grade communal depression to look like? What may paradoxically happen in a moment of crisis like this that may renew the community? If you have been a part of such an event, reflect on how the renewal of the community came about.

RELATE TO SCRIPTURE

ON YOUR OWN
Read the scriptures from your Bible. Then write down your responses to the questions for each of the selections, using the context of the "commitment window" provided by this part of the guide.

IN YOUR GROUP
As the facilitator uses the focus passages and questions to guide the session, take the opportunity to express the spontaneous insights you have received. Be sure to have your Bibles with you so that you can refer to specific passages more easily.

SCRIPTURE STATEMENTS AND QUESTION CLUSTERS FOR BREADTH:

1. **The first set of scriptures will have us look at a crowd and a collectivity by reflecting on some familiar events in the life of Christ.**

    a. Read Matthew 14:13–21 and 21:1–11. Then read Matthew 26:47–55 and 27:15–25. Compare the actions of the crowd in the first two passages with their actions in the second two passages. How do these events reveal the temporary and transient aspect of a crowd's commitment? In what way is the volatile nature of a crowd revealed in verse 27:24?

b. Read Mark 7:1–15, Luke 20:19–26, and John 8:1–11. How do these passages reveal the demands that a collectivity can make? How did this collectivity of the Pharisees and scribes differ from the kind of community that Jesus wished for us? In Mark 7:6, Jesus tells us the limitation of this collectivity. What in these people is far from God? Reflect on Christ's words in Mark 7:15. What does it mean to live from the inside out? In Luke 20:21, what is ironic about this statement made by the agents sent to trap Jesus? In John 8:11 how does Jesus free rather than impose?

2. **The two familiar stories of Daniel and Stephen give other insights into the ways of collectivities. The final passage chosen for reflection shows insight into a pneumatic community versus a humanistic one.**

   a. Read Daniel 6:1–28. This story of Daniel, a Jew exiled to Babylon after the fall of Judah in 587 B.C., is well known to us. How does Daniel attempt to remain congenial in an incompatible situation? How does the collectivity of supervisors and governors view Daniel's competence? How do they show their lack of compassion? How does Daniel show his courage? What results of his witness do we find in verses 26–28?

b. Read Acts 6:1–15 and 7:1–60. The collectivity of the past is well contrasted with the growing Christian community in these passages. Reflect on verses 1–7 of Acts 6 to see how the community shows their congeniality, compatibility, compassion, and competence. How is Stephen described in verses 5 and 8? How does he courageously attempt, through the power of the Spirit, to awaken those who come to debate him? How does he show his compassion in verse 60 of Acts 7? How does he show himself to be a member of the body of Christ by his last words? Refer to Psalm 22:18 and Luke 23:34 as you reflect on Stephen's words. What do they add to your perspective?

c. Read Acts 5:17–42. Reflect on this event involving Peter and the apostles. How do verses 36–39 show, as the authors have suggested, that no human effort can pretend to build this body of Christ?

3. **The authors speak often in this part concerning the body of Christ. Some of Paul's letters are particularly illuminating in relation to this image of Christian community.**

a. Read Ephesians 4:1–32 and 5:1–20. How are building up the body of Christ and becoming spiritually mature related in verses 1–16 in chapter 4? How are Christ's words from Mark 7:6 re-echoed in 4:18? Verse 22 refers to the old self and verse 24 to the new self. What are these two selves? How does the description of a Christian community given in 4:25–32 and 5:1–20 match with the five C's that the authors present as signs of a sound Christian formation community?

b. Read Colossians 3:5–17. In this letter, Paul again compares the old self and the new self, our hidden likeness in the mystery of transforming love. Reflect on verses 14–15. Again our hearts are mentioned in these verses, only now they are no longer the hardened heart of the old self. What is Christ's gift to our heart?

c. Read 1 Corinthians 12:12–31. Paul speaks again of the one body with many parts that should characterize a Christian formation community. Why are verses 12:12–31 truly descriptive of a pneumatic community? How are the five C's also revealed in these verses?

RECORD YOUR DIALOGUE

ON YOUR OWN
Record that which touches your life, that which inspires you and deepens your awareness of your life direction in the light of your commitment to your own specific Christian faith and formation tradition.

IN THE GROUP
If your group has decided to allot a short time for notebook sharing, you may, if you wish, offer insights that might benefit the other members of the group.

RECLAIM THE CLASSICS

ON YOUR OWN
Read over the following annotated suggestions for further reading. Reflect on the glimpses given to see which classics you might like to "reclaim."

Benedict, St. *The Rule of St. Benedict.* Trans. Abbot Justin McCann. London: Sheed and Ward, 1972.

    Through St. Benedict and his order, the essentials of western civilization were preserved amid the chaos and confusion of the dark ages. The Rule, which he established for his monks, and which for centuries has been a source of spiritual reading, has had an influence extending far beyond the cloisters of his own community. This text is of service and interest not only to the monk but also to the general reader, for it addresses any who choose to follow Christ's way of presence to the Father in a community of love.

Boros, Ladislaus. *Meeting God in Man.* Trans. William Glen-Doepel. Garden City, N.Y.: Doubleday, Image Books, 1971.

    The key to holiness lies in the fullest possible unfolding of our graced humanity. By presenting a fresh approach to traditional values, Boros emphasizes that we reach God by meeting the mystery in our brothers and sisters. The model for this meeting is Christ, whose life on earth is the most perfect example of how to attain true holiness by knowing, loving, and identifying with other pilgrims on the way.

Francis of Assisi, St. *The Little Flowers of St. Francis.* Trans. Raphael Brown. Garden City, N.Y.: Doubleday & Co., Inc., 1958.

    Francis' warmth and gaiety radiate in the best-loved stories of the Poverello and his followers: his sermon to the birds, the stigmata, the wolf of Gubbio, the preaching of St. Anthony, the soaring "Canticle of Brother Sun," the lives and sayings of Brothers Juniper and Giles. Above all, this is the story of how the Little Poor Man taught the world about the love of Christ and how this love can be lived and enjoyed by everyone.

Julian of Norwich. *Showings.* Trans. Edmund Colledge, O.S.A. New York: Paulist Press, 1978.

Revelations given to an anchoress living in fourteenth century England, these sixteen "showings" of God's love offer us a warm and simple reflection on communion with the Trinity, on our share in the divine plan. Expressed in a language at once humorous and profound, perennial truths concerning sin, grace, redemption, the humanity of Christ, and the motherly mercy of God the Father are presented with a quiet humility by one who knew from experience that God dwells among us.

Thérèse of Lisieux. *The Autobiography of St. Thérèse of Lisieux: The Story of a Soul.* Trans. John Beevers. Garden City, N.Y.: Doubleday, Image Books, 1957.

This moving autobiography recounts the story of the saint's struggle to use her limitations to reach the heights of sanctity. It was she who asked God to take her nothingness and transform it into living fire. Writing under obedience to her superiors, Thérèse tells in journal form the story of a highly sensitive young woman who lets God draw strength from her weakness and through the purifying trials of communal participation. Thérèse's mission, despite her many physical, emotional, and spiritual setbacks, was to make God loved as God deserves to be loved and to teach the Christian community the "little way" of spiritual childhood.

van Kaam, Adrian. *Living Creatively.* Denville, N.J.: Dimension Books, 1978.

This is an experiential study of the leveling tendency that threatens to stifle originality. It describes the plight of the original person in a culture prone to foster conformity at the expense of true community. Creative, self-motivated people, who discover and attempt to embody in the world their ability to be themselves in a unique way, will frequently meet with destructive envy in others. This book is thus a source of encouragement for those who refuse to compromise uniqueness and originality in a functional society, who aspire, by contrast, to embody in the world the fullness of their vocation.

—— and Susan Muto. *Tell Me Who I Am*. Denville, N.J.: Dimension Books, 1977.

Many Christians today seek trustworthy direction to help them cope with rapidly changing social values without losing touch with their deepest selves. This text addresses the questions to which this search gives rise, including life in community, self-acceptance, commitment, prayer, personal feelings, and religious formation. A well-balanced initiation into the art and discipline of spiritual self-direction, the book offers wise guidance to all who seek consonance with the divine mystery of formation revealed in a field of unique and communal meaning.

PART 5

Commitment and Human Work

ADVANCE PREPARATION
Before beginning this division of the formation guide, be sure that you have read Part Five, Chapters 16, 17, 18, 19, 20, 21, and 22 of the original text.

GOAL

ON YOUR OWN
Read over the goal and consider its meaning for your own life.

IN YOUR GROUP
After opening prayer, begin the session with the facilitator reading, or asking someone else to read, the goal for this gathering.

GOAL
To examine the obstacles to and the facilitating conditions for being a committed Christian presence in the workplace.

RETURN TO THE MESSAGE

ON YOUR OWN

Consider the following key words and phrases, relating their message to your own situation. Copy some of the related passages you spontaneously marked using the extra space provided, and add any key words and phrases not already on the list.

IN YOUR GROUP

As the facilitator guides this portion of your small group session, offer your thoughts on some of the words and phrases that were especially meaningful to you.

1. *Split in Christian Consciousness*

- For many centuries faith and work had formed a natural unity; the work of cultivation, protection and celebration of this world by all social groups was lived as a "liturgy."
- By the end of the tenth century, European laity first began to experience a serious split between their everyday commitment to new kinds of social labor and their commitment to the life of the Spirit.
- The new mass of lay Christians formed by the labor force of the burghers at the beginning of the thirteenth century experienced themselves as citizens of a world that seemed to be increasingly at odds with a wholistic vision of society.
- Because of the politics of power, the division widened between the clergy who seemed to possess the church exclusively and the laity who "owned the worlds of labor, commerce, law and science."

Your Thoughts:

2. Effects of the Split

- The necessity of turning against the political and monetary interests of the clergy in order to gain freedom of labor in the realm of commerce contributed to the feeling of laity that one's actions were at odds with one's religious conscience.
- The conflict of conscience, sharpened by a preoccupation with death and damnation hovering over western humanity from the thirteenth century on, became for many the main tie with the church.
- This guilt-ridden mentality led to a mercantile approach to reconciliation and the soothing of Christian conscience.
- It also led, especially among laboring laity in the cities and at the courts of the kings, to living a double life: pietism while in church and sinfulness while in the world of secular work and relationships.

Your Thoughts:

---

3. Integration of Work and Spirituality

- For some time now the question of how to integrate commitment to the life of the Spirit with commitment to one's secular life has been neglected by sacred circles and repressed by secular learning.
- What is needed, as tension rises in the modern world, is dialogue: secular and spiritual thinkers need to seek together the integration of work and spirituality as one of the cornerstones of the twenty-first century.

Your Thoughts:

4.   Functionalism

● One obstacle to commitment in the workplace and to the reconnecting of secular and spiritual concerns is the functionalism of the twentieth century.

● Functional"ism" is the absolutizing of a partial truth, in this case that the main values in life are measurable success, mass production and achievement, even at the expense of personal relationships.

● Most committed Christians in the west have grown up in a "doing" environment and are dominated by the pulsation to perform efficiently and effectively no matter what suffers, from health to family life.

● Christian commitment is meant to be and to remain a manifestation of human and spiritual values, sustained by relaxation, play, formation, contemplation and the appreciation of aesthetic beauty.

Your Thoughts:

---

5.   Functionalism and the Threefold Path

● Obedience implies listening to the call of God in the dynamism of daily events, but the functionalistic mind reduces it to listening to the practical details of productive life alone; it substitutes pseudo-spiritual pragmat"ism" for spiritual commitment.

● Contrary to the approach of chaste, non-violating love, the pragmatic outlook often stifles Christ-centered commitment by making production and profitableness the highest wisdom.

● Although, ideally, service complements the respectful outlook of chaste love, in a culture which overvalues the pragmatic, it is easy to violate people's integrity by forcing our projects on them as the only solutions to their problems.

● Unable to leave behind our worries and preoccupations with recognizable usefulness and responsibility, we lose the poverty of spirit that lets us taste the goodness of the small and simple things of life waiting patiently for our appreciation of them.

Your Thoughts:

_____

6. *Homogeneity and Alienation*

● We have been inclined to apply the principle of homogeneity, of managing the whole by dividing it into equal parts, not only to the organization of time and production, but also to human life as such.
● Absorption by the homogeneity of common consciousness may be one reason why some Christians never seek a personal, intimate life of presence to God.
● One of the reasons why we may be alienated from spiritual experience is that we tend to rest complacently in a common consciousness we did not appropriate and expand personally and creatively.

Your Thoughts:

_____

7. *Specialization*

● In our civilization, specialization has become an almost exclusive criterion of worth; human life is reduced to positional title, economic status, and earned degrees.
● When recognition goes less to inward commitment than to outward appearances, alienation from committed living seems to increase.
● In a society where the idea of personal value is linked to advance in the profession in which one specializes, it is difficult to be who one uniquely is.

● While specialized knowledge may respond well to certain needs, it does not offer committed laity the opportunity they also need to excel as whole persons integrated by the art and discipline of spiritual living.

Your Thoughts:

---

8.   *Specialization and the Threefold Path*

● Exclusive specialization makes obedient listening difficult; it tempts us to think that a limited insight covers the whole of reality and causes us to miss the wider vision.

● Respect for others may be diminished when we view them in terms of one specialization rather than in the light of their sacred uniqueness-within-community, which no specialized knowledge can hope to grasp and appraise in its differentiated unity and fullness.

● Unless we distance ourselves from the specialized, pragmatic meaning of things, we will not be able to live the spirit of poverty that brings out the transcendent essence of things.

Your Thoughts:

---

9.   *Cultural Obstacles to Commitment*

● **Rationalism** is the rigorous attempt to base one's entire life and every human encounter solely on insights that can be obtained by means of one facet of human reason: logical and analytical intelligence.

● While the logic of our rational mind is an excellent tool, necessary for managing life, if applied indiscriminately to all areas, it may cause us to lose touch with everyday reality.

● **Behaviorism** as a life style exalts conditioned learning—not freely chosen commitment—as the main principle of character formation.

• Foundational Christian spirituality has been supplanted in some people by a trend toward religious behaviorism or the exact execution of external codes of conduct which seem to promise a perfect incarnation of holiness.

• **Existentialism** and today's "existentialistic" mentality seems to suggest that we should actualize ourselves by following only the spontaneous experiences that flow from our everyday existing in the world.

• This "ism" does not speak about our obligation to be faithful to a God-given life call, unique form or essence that pre-dates and transcends created existence.

• **Pietism** is the attempt to substitute for the affective dimension of spirituality a vague arrangement of shallow sentiments, often unrelated to the inner calling and the corresponding commitments of a person.

• True piety, by contrast, prevents the pretense that we possess religious feelings described by others when in reality we do not, or at least not yet, experience them personally.

Your Thoughts:

---

10. Committed Christian Presence

• Participating in the workplace as genuine witnesses to Christ implies that professionals, spiritually speaking, be persons who literally "profess" through their work a sense of self-worth in Christ and a benevolent dedication to the community and the world at large.

• The transcendent dispositions of congeniality, compatibility, and compassion, together with competence, courage, and commitment, are the formation ideals that laity should try to bring to life in the workplace.

• Christian social presence at work aims to place vital energies and functional talents at the service of these transcendent attitudes and actions; to the degree that this process of spiritual transformation occurs, there need be no split between who one is in Christ and what one does.

● In the deepest sense what sustains this presence is our abandonment to the beneficial meaning of the formation mystery in faith, hope, and love; no matter what happens to us in our here and now situation, we are inclined to seek the meaning of each event within the context of the mystery undergirding and embracing all persons, places, and things.

● Each time we surrender in faith to the providential meaning of a routine event or unplanned surprise in our working day, we prevent the erosion of Christian presence and its potential depletion.

Your Thoughts:

---

11. Erosion and Depletion

● The first stage of the erosion phase is marked by a temporary but real depletion of energy, interest, altruism and other aspirations to witness to Christ in the workplace; a depreciative or deformative response may begin to show up in an attitude of indifference wherein we do exactly what we have to do not to be fired, but no more.

● A second mark of the erosion crisis is that we fall back upon routine modes of conditioned social behavior; in a deformative response, we may opt to maintain proper codes of behavior, mastering the rubrics of the apparent form appropriate to our profession.

● What occurs next is the dominance of this crisis to such a degree that we may feel lost and abandoned in meaningless routine labor that appears unimportant for our growth in the Christ form of life; in a depreciating response, a strain begins to develop between life after hours and begrudged time at work.

● Depletion begins with an initial phase of exalted aspirations and ambitions; what causes trouble is the exalted nature of our intentions insofar as these are rooted less in realistic appraisal of the situation and more in our egocentric pride-form.

● Apprehensions of dissonance recur between our exalted aspirations of what should be done and a more realistic approach to what is and can be done on basis of our skills, physical stamina and the limitations of the work environment.

Your Thoughts:

---

12. *Appraisal Disposition*

● A formative response begins with the reaffirmation of an appreciative, hope-filled abandonment to the formation mystery in prayer and reflection.

● This formative response can become our characteristic way of being with God and others when we cultivate a firm yet gentle, critical yet creative, appraisal of our life direction in relation to our unique commitment to other people and to God.

● To accept that transforming the world through work means doing the best we can within the limits of any given situation tempers illusions of perfectionism as well as the expectation that life will proceed according to our plans.

● The appraisal disposition inclines us to look for the spiritual significance of everything that happens to us; it implies believing that there is a hidden providential meaning in all that transpires in our professional situation.

● To maintain this abandonment option, we must open ourselves again and again to God in faith, hope, and love, be comfortable with the tension between congeniality and compatibility, and live compassionately with the pull between our limited abilities and the given, also limited, opportunities and demands within which our life and labor unfold.

Your Thoughts:

13. Conditions Reforming Christian Presence

● Other means of reforming Christian presence call for practical interventions that complement ongoing appraisal and facilitate reformation; discovering or rediscovering the true direction of our life's commitments is essential if we are to experience peace and joy as laity in the workplace.

● At certain junctures in life, when we are asking a basic question such as "Should I partially or totally change my style or place of labor?," we may benefit from some form of formation counseling either in common or in private.

Your Thoughts:

_____

14. Conditions Facilitating Christian Presence

● Three main dispositions facilitate our remembering that we are persons called by Christ and destined to care for one another, for the people we are committed to serve; these are empathic appreciation, expressive communication and manifest joyousness.

● **Empathic Appreciation** enables us to co-experience, at least imaginatively, what others are going through; it says in effect that we accept others as they are, that we reverence their uniqueness, that we bless their being with us.

● **Expressive Communication** is the capacity, which remains underdeveloped in most of us, to be mindful of the need others feel for sincere, openhearted expression, for being listened to and understood.

● **Manifest Joyousness** is a transcendent attitude which can be felt even when we do not experience much that is fulfilling functionally speaking or gratifying vitally; it is spontaneous; it cannot be forced; it wells up from deep within our soul and may only be explicable in the light of appreciative abandonment to the formation mystery as benevolent.

● The more these dispositions become second nature to us, the more our professional and social presence will radiate the goodness, truth, and beauty characteristic of lay Christian formation.

Your Thoughts:

---

15. Repletion Sessions

● Due to the demands made upon laity in their social service and professional obligations, repletion becomes not a luxury for an elite few but a survival measure for all.

● Formative renewal sessions should be designed to help lay people get in touch with their experiences in the workplace so that they can better understand the phases of the erosion-depletion cycle in their life.

● The distinctive character of repletion sessions is that they help people develop the inner and the outer conditions necessary to foster a more congenial, compatible, compassionate, and competent Christian presence.

Your Thoughts:

Other Key Words and Phrases:

REFLECT UPON THE MEANING

ON YOUR OWN
Complete the following exercise. Where would you locate yourself between the two extremes for each of the following continuums? Put an X at the place representing you at this time in your spiritual life. Reflect on why you are at this point, and consider if this is an area in which you could benefit by being open to spiritual growth.

EXERCISE ON YOUR OWN:

1. |————————————————————————————|

See the integration of work
and spirituality as
much needed today

See the integration of
work and spirituality
as unnecessary
today

2. |————————————————————————————|

See the cultural "isms"
as stumbling blocks to the
integration of commitment to
work and our commitment to God

See the
cultural "isms" as
no barrier
to the integration
of commitment to
work and our
commitment to
God

3. |————————————————————————————|

See being
a Christian presence
in today's workplace as
an appropriate and important
effort to undertake in my
life

See being a genuine
witness and a Christian
presence in today's
workplace as an
inappropriate and
an unimportant effort
to undertake in my life

4. _____

| Respond in appreciative, hope-filled abandonment to the the formation mystery and accept that transforming the world through work means doing the best I can within the limits of any given situation | Resist responding in appreciative hope-filled abandonment to the formation mystery and am unwilling to accept that transforming the world through work means doing the best I can within the limits of any given situation |

ON YOUR OWN

Reflect upon the following discussion statements and subsequent questions. Then write in your responses in the space provided. To enhance your grasp of this aspect of self-direction, you may want to refer to the original text or the *Return to the Message* section of this guide.

IN YOUR GROUP

As the facilitator guides this portion of the session, try to offer some personal reflections on the questions.

DISCUSSION STATEMENTS AND QUESTION CLUSTERS FOR DEPTH:

1. **In Part 5, the authors help us to understand the split between commitment to work and to God by sketching the history in which work consciousness in Christian laity was formed.**

   a. What are some of the historical events that contributed to the split in Christian consciousness?

b. What effect did a guilt-ridden mentality have on the way laity came to approach the church? Describe the "double life" effect of the split that developed. In what way, if any, do aspects of these two effects still linger today? Which, if either, do you experience personally in some way?

c. What other symptoms of the split between commitment to work and to God do you see manifested today in our culture? Consider your own experience in integrating faith and work. Do they seem to be integrated or does it seem as if a split, a disintegration, exists? What are the effects in your own life of either this experienced integration or split? What feelings does living either this integrated or split existence engender in you personally?

d. The authors suggest that the integration of work and spirituality needs to be one of the cornerstones of the twenty-first century. Why is integrating work and spirituality, connecting our everyday life and our commitment in the workplace with our longing to serve God, so important? If we were able to live again faith and work as a kind of "liturgy," what would that look like in our culture? What would it look like in your own life?

2. **The authors help us to better see and understand certain obstacles in our current culture that reinforce the split and block our graced capacity to reconnect secular and spiritual concerns. They look at functionalism, homogeneity, and specialization.**

   a. How do the authors define functionalism? What does this "ism" suggest is the main value in life? What effects of a "doing" mentality do you see present in our culture? What are the potential hazards or limits to such an approach to life? What effect has being brought up in an environment dominated by a "doing" pulsation had on your own life?

   b. In what way has the cultural pulsation of functionalism influenced your listening obediently to the call of God in the dynamism of daily events? Why is it easy to violate a person's integrity in a culture that overvalues the pragmatic? Do you personally find it easy or difficult to approach others with chaste, non-violating love in a culture that values functionalism? Do you find it easy or difficult to leave behind worries and preoccupations with recognizable usefulness? Easy or difficult to live in poverty of spirit in such a utilitarian climate? Why is this so for you?

c. What do the authors suggest happens when we apply the principle of homogeneity to human life? What is a "common consciousness?" Why might a common consciousness that we did not appropriate and expand personally and creatively be one of the reasons that we are alienated from spiritual experience in our culture today? What are the effects you have personally experienced, if any, of the "cradle Christian" kind of mentality, where people have not appropriated or expanded personally their spiritual life?

d. How do the authors define specialization? What in human life becomes personally valued in a civilization where specialization is an almost exclusive criterion of worth? In your own immediate situation, how much or how little do you see people "buying into" these as the value of one's worth? In what way do these values reduce human life to a useful commodity only? What wider vision do they lose sight of?

3. **The authors touch upon four other trends in western civilization that seem detrimental to the ongoing formation of laity, especially in the workplace. They suggest that rationalism, behaviorism, existentialism, and pietism may prevent us from participating in the workplace as genuine witnesses to Christ.**

a. What does rationalism emphasize? What does it neglect? What happens when rationalism becomes the guiding principle of life in social institutions? In what way is this "ism" a part of your own approach to life? In what way can it help or hamper one's growth in spiritual maturity, in being committed to one's underlying call to God, self, and others?

b. What does behaviorism exalt as the main principle of character formation? What do the authors suggest that foundational Christian spirituality has been supplanted by in some people? What must training in externals be complemented by if growth in spiritual maturity is to take place?

c. What trend in contemporary culture do the authors relate to existential"ism"? What does this mentality tempt us to deny? In what ways do you see this self-actualizing mentality manifested in your own life? What does such a view have a tendency to neglect in regard to Christian life formation? Why do the authors say that the real source of our dignity is our God-given life call? In what ways is this self"ism" a stumbling block to the discipleship of the threefold path and to the spiritual maturation of genuinely committed Christians?

d.   How do the authors distinguish between piet"ism" and true piety or spirituality? What signs of this "ism" do you see in our culture? In what way can pietism block graced transformation on a deeper level? How do sanctimonious sentiments differ from graced inspirations? Why does pietism fail us in crisis situations?

4.   **The authors help us to see what a committed Christian presence looks like in the workplace and describe the appraisal disposition needed to prevent the erosion of Christian presence and its possible depletion.**

a.   Consider what it means to you to be a genuine witness to Christ in the workplace. What dispositions do the authors suggest can facilitate this kind of presence? Recall your earlier reflection on these dispositions from Part 4. In what way can these dispositions help you personally to be and become a Christian presence? In the deepest sense, what sustains this presence?

b.   What are the signs of erosion and subsequent depletion of Christian presence as described by the authors? To what degree and in what way are these signs present in your immediate work situation? How prevalent are they in your own life?

c. What is involved in responding formatively to the possible erosion or depletion of Christian presence in the workplace? What is the starting place for being able to appraise our life direction? What can the appraisal disposition facilitate our being able to do? Why is this kind of acceptance difficult for many in today's culture? Do you personally find this kind of formative response easy or difficult? Why has it been so for you?

5. **The authors suggest that other means of reforming committed Christian presence call for practical interventions that complement ongoing appraisal and facilitate reformation. They also present three main dispositions that facilitate the aim in the workplace of being persons called by Christ destined to care for one another.**

a. What is a basic question we must sometimes ask as a practical intervention? Why is it often a difficult question for us to consider? In what way might formation counseling be beneficial at such junctures of life? Reflect on your own life in relation to a time when you were at just such a juncture. What was the situation? What did you do? What was the outcome of your decision?

b. What three dispositions do the authors introduce that facilitate our being in the workplace as persons called by Christ who are committed to serve? Which of these dispositions comes most naturally to you? Which seems to be the most illusive for you? In what way and to what degree are these dispositions a part of Christian presence in the workplace? In what way do they differ from the use of humanistic techniques?

c. What is manifest joyousness? How does transcendent, spiritual joy manifest itself? Reflect on a time in your own experience when you were graced with manifest joyousness in the midst of a situation that was not fulfilling functionally or gratifying vitally. What was the source of that joy? How did that joy manifest itself in you? What effect did your own joy have on those around you?

d. What are repletion sessions? Why do the authors suggest that they are not a luxury, but a survival measure for all? Why is it important that they be ongoing? Why does dealing with defor-mation take a lifetime? Why do we always have to resource ourselves in the sustaining strength of the Spirit if we seek to live as committed Christians on the way to ever deepening spiritual maturity? How is that possible? What kind of resources exist in your immediate situation for such formative renewal? In what way have these direction-in-common sessions, reflecting on the *Commitment* text, become a source of repletion?

RELATE TO SCRIPTURE

ON YOUR OWN

Read the scriptures from your Bible. Then write down your responses to the questions for each of the selections, using the context of the "commitment window" provided by this part of the guide.

IN YOUR GROUP

As the facilitator uses the focus passages and questions to guide the session, take the opportunity to express the spontaneous insights you have received. Be sure to have your Bibles with you so that you can refer to specific passages more easily.

SCRIPTURE STATEMENTS AND QUESTION CLUSTERS FOR BREADTH:

1. **Throughout the book the authors have helped us see our unique, underlying call to commitment as the core that unifies all aspects of our lived existence, whether in marriage, singleness, or as a member of a community. In Part 5, the authors help us to recognize the natural unity between our faith and our work, between who we most deeply are in Christ and what we do. They stress the importance of reconnecting or integrating every aspect of our life, including our commitment to work, with our deepest call to commitment to God.**

    a. Read Exodus 31:1–11; 35:30–35; 36:1–7. In chapter 31, we see the unity of natural abilities, one's work and one's unique call. What about the importance of this integration do the Lord's words to Moses concerning the craftsmen in chapter 31 help us to recognize? Reflect upon verse 2 in chapter 36, perhaps even reading its wording in more than one translation. How does this line reinforce the aspect of choice or freedom to be faithful that are ours in following our call? How do verses 4 to 7 in chapter 36 communicate to us the wise use of things, or poverty of spirit, that these craftsmen exercised?

b. Read John 4:34; 5:17, 36; 6:37–38; 9:4–5; 12:23–24; 14:10–11; 17:4. Christ's call was the most unique of all. How do the words of Jesus recorded in John's gospel reveal the unity of one's call and one's work? What do they suggest is the relationship between one's unique call, the works one is to accomplish, and the will of God? When, do they suggest, is one's unique call established?

c. Read Matthew 12:15–21 and Colossians 1:15–20. In Matthew 12:18 we find that Jesus was chosen for what role as foretold by the prophet Isaiah? How did that contrast with the role of earthly king that even his apostles thought for a while he was to fulfill? What additional insight about Christ's unique call is made clear by the words of Paul in his letter to the Colossians?

d.   Read Acts 9:10–19; 22:12–16; 1 Corinthians 15:8–11; Galatians 1:15. The details concerning Paul's unique call to commitment abound in his letters as well as in the book of Acts. The Lord uses people, things, and events in our lives as directives pointing to our call. In Acts 9, whom has the Lord used to reveal Paul's call to him? What disposition is suggested by 1 Corinthians 15:9? In verse 15:10, what does Paul attribute to his being as he is? What does verse 1:15 in Galatians tell us about when Paul's unique call was established? In Acts 22:15, what does Paul describe his call as doing?

e.   Read Ephesians 3:1–12 and Colossians 1:25–29. What secret does Paul reveal to us in both of these passages? How is this secret related to the work that he was called to do? What disposition of Paul's is again suggested by Ephesians 3:8? How does he refer to himself in 3:7 and 1:25?

f. Read John 14:11–17; 15:8–10, 16–17; Galatians 5:22–25. Christ speaks of our unique call and the work we are to do. In John 14:11–12, what is the condition Jesus gives for our being able to be true to our unique call? What are we given in verse 14:26 to facilitate our graced transformation? What in verse 14:27 can we experience as we discover and rediscover the true direction of our life call to commitment? In John 15:8–10, 16–17, what are we told will give witness to our being true to the unique call of the Christ form within us which was ours from all eternity? What fruits of the life lived in the Spirit are given in Galatians 5:13–25? What is the only way in which we are able to grow in these fruits? How is becoming rich in them related to our growing in spiritual maturity?

g. Read 1 Corinthians 15:58 and Colossians 3:23–24. Paul also speaks of the unity of our unique call and our work. What work in 1 Corinthians does he tell us to stay busy in or devoted to? Why is his reassurance in verse 58 important to us? Recall a time in your own life when that reassurance had personal significance. What was the situation? Why was the reassurance needed? How did you receive it? How did receiving it make you feel? In Colossians 3:23–24, what are we reminded must be at the heart of all our work? Whom is it we serve?

2. **The authors help us consider some of the obstacles to Christian commitment with which we are faced, especially in the workplace. They suggest that Christian professionals, spiritually speaking, are**

persons who literally "profess" through their work a sense of self-worth in Christ and a benevolent dedication to the community and the world at large.

a. Read Luke 12:13–21 and Matthew 20:1–16. What aspect of functionalism is touched upon in these verses from Luke 12? Consider verse 12:21. What does it look like to be rich in God's sight? In what way does the story in Matthew contradict some of the absolutizing of functional"ism"? What about this story might be uncomfortable for some people?

b. Read Revelation 3:14–22. Reflect on this message to one of the seven cities in view of what the authors say about homogeneity and common consciousness. What is lacking in the common consciousness of the people of this city? How does verse 17 show the influence of functionalistic thought? What well-known image does verse 20 bring to mind? Who is knocking? At what door does he knock?

c. Read Matthew 20:20–28 and Mark 10:35–45. What criterion of worth that the authors associate with specialization is evidenced in this story? How does this help us to see that even the apostles were not clear concerning the real mission of Christ's unique life call until after his death and resurrection?

d. Read Matthew 16:24–28; Mark 8:34–38; Luke 9:23–26; John 12:23–26. Jesus' conditions for being his disciple in the world appear in all of the gospel narratives. Consider the verse in Matthew 16:26, Mark 8:36 and Luke 9:25. To which cultural obstacles current today do these words speak? What do Christ's words in Matthew 16:25, Mark 8:35, and Luke 9:24 mean to you? How is that possible? Ponder Christ's words recorded in John's gospel. What must a grain of wheat do when planted if it is to become more than a grain of wheat? What is it able to do if it dies to the form that it was? What about these words are analogous to the formation journey of our own lives? In John 12:26, what does Christ tell us we are to become? How does this relate to what you read earlier for questions 1 c and e in Matthew 12:18, Ephesians 3:7, and Colossians 1:25?

e. Read Philippians 3:4–11; Galatians 1:11–20; 2:15–21. In both Galatians 1:13–14 and Philippians 3:4–6, what does Paul tell us about himself before his call became known to him? What does he realize in Philippians 3:8 is more valuable? How has more clearly coming to know his unique call transformed his life? In Galatians 2:19–20, how are the words you just considered in John 12 echoed? Which verses tell us about the part faith and grace play in this? What is the role of grace and faith?

f. Read Ephesians 2:4–10; 2 Corinthians 5:16–21; 6:1–10. Consider what these passages say about grace and faith. In what way do the verses in 2 Corinthians echo Christ's words in Matthew 16:24, Mark 8:34, and Luke 9:23?

g. Read 1 Corinthians 1:10–31; 2:1–16. How do the verses in chapter 1 point out the limitations of rationalism discussed by the authors? How does it relate to the paradox of the cross? What wisdom does Paul say in chapter 2 of his letter is that which they teach to the spiritually mature? What is revealed to us through the spirit?

3. **The authors help us to see how the appraisal disposition can foster a formative response to life, especially in the midst of an erosion and depletion crisis. Appraisal is a more realistic approach to what is and can be done on the basis of our skills, physical stamina, and the limitations of the work environment.**

a. Read Luke 14:27–33. Appraisal helps us to accept that transforming the world through work means doing the best we can within the limits of any given situation. What two examples of appraisal does Jesus give in this passage on being his disciple? What is the cost of discipleship brought out in these verses?

b. Read Matthew 25:14–30. How does this familiar story that Jesus told illustrate the importance of the wise use of the gifts and talents one has been given? What did the two do who were faithful servants? What happens when one is not a faithful servant? In what way is this response a deformative one that the authors associate with one of the marks of an erosion crisis?

c. Read 2 Samuel 7:1–29. What do we find in verses 1 and 2 that David wants to do for God? Although perhaps a noble sentiment, what response of God is made known through the prophet Nathan? In verses 9 and 11, what do we learn is David's unique call through the grace and goodness of God? Whose unique call will it be to build the temple for God? How do David's words in verses 18–29 evidence his appreciative, hope-filled abandonment to the formation mystery in prayer and reflection? Why do you think David gave up his original plan in verse 2? Reflect on a time in your own life when you discovered that an exalted aspiration you had was not a part of your unique call in God. What was the situation? What did you discover? How did you discover it? What was your response? In what way, if any, did this event temper illusions of perfectionism or the expectation that life would proceed according to your plans?

d. Read 1 Corinthians 3:1–23; 4:1–5; 2 Corinthians 10:12–18. How does Paul's teaching in 1 Corinthians help us to see our role as one of servant and steward? Who causes the growth when one waters and another plants? What is the only foundation on which one can build? In 2 Corinthians 10:13 and 15, how does Paul evidence the appraisal disposition that accepts transforming the world through work means doing the best we can within the limits of any given situation?

4. **The authors help us to see what a committed Christian presence looks like and remind us of what dispositions facilitate our call by Christ to care for one another. They help us recall that we must open ourselves again and again to God in faith, hope, and love to sustain this presence.**

a. Read Matthew 5:14–16; Philippians 2:1–18; 2 Timothy 2:1–25. What image for committed Christian presence does Jesus give us in these verses in Matthew? How does Paul add to and expand upon that image in Philippians 2? What image of the kenotic Christ is found in verse 7? Which dispositions for facilitating Christian presence are alluded to in those verses? How does this confirm what the authors told us that these dispositions make possible? Reflect on what ways you serve as a light for others as a committed Christian? Is being a light in the workplace something that you find easy or difficult? What do you think makes it so? In 2 Timothy 2:15–17 and 22–25, what characteristic way of being with God and with others does Paul encourage Timothy to follow and teach? Which dispositions are alluded to in these verses? Consider the image of dishes that Paul gives in verses 21 and 22. What is his message to us here?

b.   Read 1 Thessalonians 1:1–7; Ephesians 1:15–18; Galatians 5:6; 1 Corinthians 13:13; Romans 5:1–8. The authors stress that what sustains a committed Christian presence is abandoning ourselves to the beneficial meaning of the formation mystery in faith, hope, and love. Reflect upon the message concerning faith, hope, and love in each of these passages from Paul's letters.

c.   Read John 14:27; 15:11; 17:13, Romans 14:17–19; Philippians 4:4–13; 1 Peter 1:1–9. The authors tell us that manifest joyousness is a transcendent attitude that may be felt even when we do not experience much that is fulfilling functionally speaking or gratifying vitally. In John 14 and 15, what is the source of our joy and peace that makes it a transcendent attitude? In Romans 14, what does Paul say is the source of our peace and joy? In Philippians 4, what is the source of the joy? What gift beyond our understanding is given to us? Who gives it? What attitude mentioned here, as in 2 Timothy 2:25, should we show toward others? In Philippians 4:10–13, what has Paul learned is his source of renewal and repletion? Recall a time in your life when these words of Paul's rang true for you. What was the situation? How did you feel? What made that possible? What additional insights concerning our joy does 1 Peter 1:1–9 give us? How do these verses help us to see that repletion is a survival measure for all?

RECORD YOUR DIALOGUE

ON YOUR OWN
Record that which touches your life, that which inspires you and deepens your awareness of your life direction in the light of your commitment to your own specific Christian faith and formation tradition.

IN THE GROUP
If your group has decided to allot a short time for notebook sharing, you may, if you wish, offer insights that might benefit the other members of the group.

RECLAIM THE CLASSICS

ON YOUR OWN
Read over the following annotated suggestions for further reading. Reflect on the glimpses given to see which classics you might like to "reclaim."

de Sales, Francis, St. *Introduction to the Devout Life*. Trans. Michael Day. New York: E.P. Dutton and Co., Everyman's Library, 1961.

   Francis addresses readers who, to all outward appearances, lead an ordinary life, but who, within their limits, aspire to a high degree of devotion. He believes there is an unbreakable bond between the sacred and the secular. The integration of work and prayer is essential to the devout life as Francis describes it, for Christians are called with their entire being to embody God's love while participating in the affairs of this world.

Hammarskjöld, Dag. *Markings*. Trans. Leif Sjöberg and W.H. Auden. New York: Alfred A. Knopf, 1969.

   The diary of an intensely dedicated public servant, *Markings* profiles Hammarskjöld's gradual discovery of what it means to say "yes" to one's neighbor and one's fate, first as a civil servant in his homeland, Sweden, and then as secretary-general of the United Nations. Hammarskjöld remained single throughout his life; he saw himself as a man with a mission—to be a servant of peace in a hostile, power-hungry world. Though Dag wrote for himself and not for the public, the resulting collection can be read, in his words, ". . . as a sort of *white book* concerning my negotiations with myself—and with God."

Kelly, Thomas R. *A Testament of Devotion*. New York: Harper & Row, Publishers, 1941.

   Kelly's book is an ideal companion to that highest of human arts, the lifelong conversation with God and us that occurs during work and prayer. In the five essays of the *Testament*—"The Light Within," "Holy Obedience," "The Blessed Community," "The Eternal Now and Social Concern," and "The Simplification of Life" —there emerges a clear-cut path through the underbrush of day-to-day worries and frustrations into the cool glades of spiritual peace. Like St. Francis de Sales, Kelly proves that the functional realm is a servant of the transcendent, that doing must not be separated from devotion.

Lawrence of the Resurrection, Brother. *The Practice of the Presence of God.* Trans. Donald Attwater. Springfield, Ill.: Templegate, 1974.
 Brother Lawrence tells of a spirituality within reach of all because it is based on the practice of ceaseless prayer, cultivated by a sense of the presence of God alive at each moment of ordinary life, in the kitchen cleaning pots and pans as well as in the chapel. The author shows how any properly disposed person can consecrate his or her life, however uneventful it may seem, to the ever-present God. Such "practice" leads us from the mundane to the sublime with ease; it enables us to pray always, whether we are at work or play, doing chores or calming our minds in silent contemplation.

Nouwen, Henri J.M. *The Wounded Healer: Ministry in Contemporary Society.* Garden City, N.Y.: Doubleday, Image Books, 1979.
 Noting that modern people are suffering from lack of hope, from loneliness and the predicament of rootlessness, the author holds that ministers or healers can only help others if they are willing to go beyond professional roles and open themselves as human beings to their own wounds and suffering. Nouwen suggests concrete methods by which healers can bring freedom and liberation to people afflicted by physical and emotional disease. He suggests, based on his own experience, that only those who have been wounded can understand and respond to another person's cry for wholeness and healing.

Oates, Wayne E. *Confessions of a Workaholic.* New York: Abingdon Press, 1971.
 In an honest, lively way, Oates recounts his own addiction to work and how he had to reform. After discussing the origin of workaholism, its social, religious and emotional influences, the author identifies symptoms that show up prior to addiction and offers practical suggestions for placing work in a new, more satisfying, and

fulfilling perspective. This book confirms the necessity of changing a pattern of life which consumes far more than it produces in those who are trapped in it.

van Kaam, Adrian. *Dynamics of Spiritual Self-Direction*. Denville, N.J.: Dimension Books, 1976.

How can we discover the unique self-direction God wants for our life? The author answers this question by discussing several related issues, including the connection between self-alienation and self-emergence. He discloses in detail the dynamics of spiritual direction and the proper time and place for one-on-one or private direction as practiced in the church. To integrate commitment to Christ and competence in one's work is not easy. Such matters call for repeated appraisal, but the effort is worth it if we want to discover the key to happiness, consonance with the divine direction of our life.

PART 6

Commitment
and Prayerful Living
as Laity

ADVANCE PREPARATION
Before beginning this division of the formation guide, be sure that you have read Part Six, Chapters 23, 24, and 25 of the original text.

GOAL

ON YOUR OWN
Read over the goal and consider its meaning for your own life.

IN YOUR GROUP
After opening prayer, begin the session with the facilitator reading, or asking someone else to read, the goal for this gathering.

GOAL
To show that spiritual disciplines and a life of prayer keep our lives oriented toward our deeper calling and commitment.

RETURN TO THE MESSAGE

ON YOUR OWN
Consider the following key words and phrases, relating their message to your own situation. Copy some of the related passages you spontaneously marked using the extra space provided, and add any key words and phrases not already on the list.

IN YOUR GROUP
As the facilitator guides this portion of your small group session, offer your thoughts on some of the words and phrases that were especially meaningful to you.

---

1. *Daily Deepening*

- Striving for a life of spiritual deepening in the midst of daily living means that we must be willing to confront obstacles in the life of work and prayer that hinder or delay us on our journey to God.
- Simultaneously, we must create conditions that facilitate our capacity to seek a more harmonious presence to the formation mystery.

Your Thoughts:

---

2. *Spiritual Frigidity*

- Spiritual frigidity appears to be rooted in an unconscious attitude of protest and resistance acquired in childhood and adolescence; it connotes an inability to respond creatively to what God allows to occur in one's life.
- People who are spiritually frigid fear religious experiences of any kind and are unable to surrender to anything that calls for risk and the relinquishing of control.

• Lacking the power or potency to surrender to the mystery in an appreciatively abandoned manner, they are unable to cling in deep faith to God even in midnight moments of not understanding; thus, they fail to receive the peace that only God can give.

• With God's grace, a well-prepared formation counselor can assist in releasing people of good will from the immobilizing grip of spiritual frigidity.

Your Thoughts:

---

3. *Overcoming Spiritual Frigidity*

• Married or single persons must sense and feel their own resistant emotions to anything associated with spirituality by allowing depreciative fears and frigid responses to come to the surface of their consciousness.

• For healing to occur, one must become aware that such deep and hidden fears about religion and spirituality are shaped early in life; they are in great measure defenses against fixations and confusions in the realm of religion and do not pertain to spirituality in the formative sense.

• With the help of grace, we may dare to allow depreciative, frigid feelings and their underlying emotions to lessen their power over us so that we can at least be free to know and love God as we desire.

• Grace precedes and fosters the healing of our interiority; it flows freely through a committed Christian heart ready to receive its transforming influence.

Your Thoughts:

4. Avenues to Committed Living

● For Christians willing to search courageously and to expose to light lingering deformative dispositions, there is much hope; it is just such a purification process that prepares us to comprehend and embrace a life of prayer and spiritual abandonment as essential steps along the way to Christian maturity.

● The longer we live, the more we sense our need for God's grace to sustain us in our quest to be committed lay Christians; as avenues to maturity in faith, we may pursue in cooperation with grace certain disciplines that help us to meet God in everyday life.

Your Thoughts:

---

5. Formative or Spiritual Reading

● Spiritual reading is a foundational exercise that prepares us for committed Christian living; it returns us to the classics of our faith tradition while readying us for Christian service in a diversity of new and challenging situations.

● This kind of reading requires that we become disciples of the word of God as it addresses us through the faith-filled words of scripture, the church fathers, and classical and contemporary masters.

● This formative approach asks that we adopt the dispositions of a disciple rather than the attitudes of mastery characteristic of one who gathers information only.

Your Thoughts:

6. Dispositions Fostering Receptivity

- **Rumination** is the disposition by which we savor the wisdom of the text, returning to it again and again, hoping to grow in intimacy with God.
- **Dwelling** is the spiral movement by which we move slowly from one sentence to another, resting in any that appeals to our spirit and letting our mind and heart sink into its meaning.
- **Docility** is the spirit by which we listen with our inner ear attuned to the silent whispers of the Spirit; in docility we open ourselves to the guidance the Spirit may grant to us in regular sessions of personal or shared reading.

Your Thoughts:

---

7. Knowing with the Heart

- The discursive aspect of the intellect is highly developed in the west; it facilitates logical reasoning and information sciences, but in and by itself it cannot grasp the full significance of spiritual texts as life messages.
- Being with a message in a reflective state of wonder, awe, and adoration is when scripture and spiritual masters come alive for us; this is the means by which we pierce through the knowledge gained by the logical intellect to another level of reason where we are open to the mystery.
- Beyond the information that comes through the discursive intellect, we discover in an experiential way what it is like to live in the awareness of God's presence that transcends explanatory effort; living in the wonder of paradox and unknowing that fosters humility, we learn that the gift of enlightenment is beyond our power of control.
- It is this knowledge of the heart that the church fathers and spiritual masters want to communicate so that we, their readers, can

come to a more personal living of the mystery and majesty of our faith; they seek not so much to explain these mysteries of faith as to show us how to live them.

Your Thoughts:

_____

8. Seeing in Faith

● It is through the formative reading of scriptures and the classic and contemporary masters of spirituality that we begin to see in faith; we begin the never-ending process of becoming servants of the word.

● As we develop and deepen, as we open ourselves more and more to God's grace alive and at work in us, the words we read may be the same, but their meaning is different; the text begins to disclose its secrets to us.

● Even texts that seemed easy to understand at first may become more paradoxical; the faith we took for granted challenges us anew.

● God becomes a "dazzling darkness," but how can the darkness be dazzling? The Spirit speaks in silence, but how can silence speak?

Your Thoughts:

_____

9. Remaining Simple in a Complex World

● As we begin to orient everything we say or do or think around the themes of committed living, so well articulated in scripture and the spiritual classics, we begin to wholly trust in the Lord, to serve God in purity of heart and poverty of spirit, and to remain simple in a complex world.

● In a world that fosters the compulsion to read everything, we simplify by perhaps choosing, in addition to holy scripture, one or two spiritual writers who really speak to us.

- In a world full of noise, we value silence and slowed down reading.
- We keep in mind the real meaning of our life call as laity: to witness in the everyday world of family, leisure, and labor to the basic truths of spiritual deepening and to communicate by our life what we have heard of God.

Your Thoughts:

_____

10. Practice of Prayer

- Prayer opens the door to the gift of divine transforming love awaiting us.
- Although there are many ways in which we can learn to pray, the important thing is to follow the way the Spirit leads us.
- Some say that to pray is to learn to talk to God; others teach that it is a conversation; still others suggest it is meditation on the love and knowledge of God, or a reflection on our life while turning our hearts to the holy.
- Whatever way is ours, what matters is to develop a personal love relationship with God; to be silent together; to enjoy being close.

Your Thoughts:

_____

11. Prayer of Presence

- A deeper way of learning to pray is to try to live in the presence of God, to pray always as the gospel writers and St. Paul in his epistles recommend.
- As we develop this disposition, awareness of God's presence becomes an underlying theme of our life, an undercurrent of our stream of consciousness that never leaves us totally.

● This way of prayer implies making room in our heart for the experience of God's loving presence deep within us and all around us.

Your Thoughts:

_____

12. *Moments of Stillness*

● Remaining in God's presence is the condition of always praying.
● Jesus himself gave the example by time and again creating moments of stillness in his life to be alone with God; this abiding in his Father was nourished by the words of the Hebrew scriptures on which he had meditated since his youth.
● To follow Jesus' life of prayer, we need to pay attention to God's words; when a passage strikes us as personally meaningful or fills us with peace, we should treasure it in our hearts, take it with us in our daily life, and return to it again and again.
● Steadily returning to the words of the Lord, of disciples, of church fathers, of saints and spiritual writers keeps our life oriented toward our deeper calling and commitment; we, too, begin to truly abide in God.
● Even if we do not feel the effects of this dwelling, we can be sure that in time God will grant us momentary illuminations, brief glimpses, passing but real experiences of a Presence beyond words.
● In the end we may receive the grace of praying always; we may have found the key to commitment, the key to Christian maturity.

Your Thoughts:

_____

Other Key Words and Phrases:

REFLECT UPON THE MEANING

ON YOUR OWN

Complete the following exercise. Where would you locate yourself between the two extremes for each of the following continuums? Put an X at the place representing you at this time in your spiritual life. Reflect on why you are at this point, and consider if this is an area in which you could benefit by being open to spiritual growth.

EXERCISE ON YOUR OWN:

1. |_____|

| Readily embrace a life of prayer and spiritual abandonment as essential steps along the way to Christian maturity | Strongly resist a life of prayer and spiritual abandonment as essential steps along the way to Christian maturity |

2. |_____|

| Able to see the importance of doing spiritual reading and seek to adopt the formative dispositions which foster receptivity to the text | Unable to see the importance of doing spiritual reading and make no effort to adopt the formative dispositions which foster receptivity to the text |

3. |_____|

| Find it very comfortable to live in the wonder of going beyond logical reasoning to the mystery and majesty of faith | Find it most uncomfortable to live in the wonder of going beyond logical reasoning to the mystery and majesty of faith |

4. |_____|

| Find it easy to conceive of the possibility of living in the presence of God, of praying always | Find it difficult to conceive of the possibility of living in the presence of God, of praying always |

Reflect upon the following discussion statements and subsequent questions. Then write your responses in the space provided. To enhance your grasp of this aspect of self-direction, you may want to refer to the original text or the *Return to the Message* section of this guide.

As the facilitator guides this portion of the session, try to offer some personal reflections on the questions.

DISCUSSION STATEMENTS AND QUESTION CLUSTERS FOR DEPTH:

1. **The authors suggest that spiritual deepening continually happens in the midst of daily living when we are willing to confront obstacles that hinder us on our journey to God and to create conditions that facilitate a more harmonious presence to the formation mystery.**

    a. Describe in your own words the obstacle of spiritual frigidity presented by the authors for consideration. In what ways may this obstacle manifest itself? In what attitudes is it usually rooted, especially in committed Christians? What basic ingredient for spiritual intimacy are they unable to receive? What are some possible rigid or restrictive ideas about God that are part of your own experience? From where, do you think, came some of these ideas? In what ways are they formative or deformative?

b. Why may some people be afraid to make the necessary inward journey to let depreciative feelings come to the fore? What are the conditions needed for healing of spiritual frigidity to occur? In what way is this a purification process? What does such "purifying" prepare us to do? Reflect on the meaning of God's grace in your life. What is grace? Why is overcoming spiritual frigidity impossible without it?

2. **The authors suggest that one of the avenues to maturity in faith is to pursue, in cooperation with grace, the discipline of formative or spiritual reading.**

a. How do the authors define formative or spiritual reading? Describe the dispositions that foster our receptivity to God's word. In what way do these contrast dramatically with approaches to reading and gathering information so prevalent in our culture today? Which, if any, of these obstacles serve as stumbling blocks to your own practice of the discipline of formative reading?

b. Why is the discursive aspect of our intellect unable to grasp in and by itself the full significance of spiritual texts as life messages? What are the dispositions necessary to pierce through the knowledge gained by our intellect? Why is the gift of enlightenment beyond our power to control? What does the expression "knowing with the heart" mean to you? What is it that you know? "How" do you know it? In what way is its meaning deeper than the ways in which today's culture tends to image the heart?

c. What happens when we begin to "see in faith" as the authors suggest? What makes such seeing possible? Who opens our eyes that we may see the unseen? What does it mean to you to become a servant of the word? What is the word? Who is the word?

d. Recall a time when something in scripture or a spiritual classic came alive for you in a new way. What was the passage that began to speak to your now "knowing heart"? What was the "in"sight that you received? What effect did receiving this inspiration have on you?

e. What part do trust and serving God in purity of heart and poverty of spirit play in being able to remain simple in a complex world? What does the phrase "purity of heart" mean to you? What makes purity of heart possible?

f. What are some of the guidelines that the authors suggest for remaining simple amid the complex? Do you experience these as easy or difficult to carry out? Why is that? What effect has their being easy or difficult to carry out had on your life? At its deepest core, how does the authors' focus on gaining integration and wholeness through these means differ from some of the seemingly similar techniques espoused in our culture today for fostering wholeness? Why is this distinction so basic?

3. **The authors tell us that prayer opens the door to the gift of divine transforming love awaiting us. It, too, is an avenue to spiritual maturity.**

a. In what way does prayer open doors? What door do you visualize it opening? What are some of the paths to prayer that others teach or advise as helpful in learning to pray? How do the authors suggest that we learn to pray? What do they say is most important to follow in the way one prays?

b. Consider your current way of prayer. How does it help you to develop a personal love relationship with God? Think of a time when you may have used the words "falling in love" to describe what was happening to you. What was the situation? How did it feel? What do you envision falling in love with God to feel like? With commitment as the key, what do you see that personal love relationship beginning to look like?

c. What do the authors mean by the expression the "prayer of presence"? To whose presence are they referring? How does such an "undercurrent of our stream of consciousness" differ from other former kinds of prayer? Why is this referred to as the condition of praying always? What means of fostering moments of stillness do the authors suggest? If you have tried this approach, what about it has proven helpful?

d. What does the word "abide" mean to you? What do you envision abiding in God to be like? Recall a time when you might have experienced such an abiding. What were the effects of this dwelling? In what way did these moments flow over into the rest of your lived existence? Why do the authors suggest that praying always may hold the key to commitment, to Christian maturity? Why is this a grace to be received rather than something we can achieve?

RELATE TO SCRIPTURE

ON YOUR OWN
Read the scriptures from your Bible. Then write down your responses to the questions for each of the selections, using the context of the "commitment window" provided by this part of the guide.

IN YOUR GROUP
As the facilitator uses the focus passages and questions to guide the session, take the opportunity to express the spontaneous insights you have received. Be sure to have your Bibles with you so that you can refer to specific passages more easily.

SCRIPTURE STATEMENTS AND QUESTION CLUSTERS FOR BREADTH:

1. **The authors say that spiritual frigidity connotes an inability to respond creatively to what God allows to occur in one's life; it is when one lacks the power or potency to surrender to the mystery in an appreciatively abandoned manner. The authors tell us that grace precedes and fosters the healing of our interiority; it flows freely through a committed Christian heart ready to receive its transforming influence.**

   a. Read Exodus 17:1–7; Psalm 95:8–11; Hebrews 3:1–18; 4:1–11. These passages all relate to the resistance or "hardened hearts" of those Moses led out of Egypt. In what way did the Israelite community put God to the test at Massah and Meribah? What is it that they were demanding from God? How does the incident, which is one of many in the desert story, show the people's inability to respond creatively to what God allowed to occur? What caution are we given by the author of Hebrews in verse

3:12? What does he say must be done to safeguard against that? In verses 3:18–19, what is it that the people were unable to receive? Why were they unable to receive it? What is the rest that we are promised in Hebrews 4:9–10? Why is the healing of spiritual frigidity so important?

b. Read John 4:1–42. This woman at the well was ready to receive the transforming influence of grace that is necessary for over-coming spiritual frigidity. By whom was it offered? What was offered to the woman that had also been given to the Israelites in the story above? In what way does it differ from that which was offered to them? In verses 23 and 24, what does Jesus explain will make true worship of the heart possible? How does Jesus show that he knows the truth of what is in the woman's heart? In what way does she become an effective witness for Jesus?

c. Read Hebrews 7:15–28; 8:1–13; 10:15–23; Jeremiah 31:31–37; Ezekiel 36:26–28. What promises of God foretold by the prophets Jeremiah and Ezekiel are mentioned in Hebrews 8:10–12 and 10:15–16? Who arranged this covenant for us? How is it superior to the old covenant? What is the better hope by which we may draw near to God? Reflect on Hebrews 10:19–23. What do the verses suggest to you is possible?

d. Read Ephesians 1:15–23. What is the prayer that Paul prays on our behalf? What does he request that we receive? How could this help people overcome spiritual frigidity? What is it that Paul prays that we will see or come to know in our heart?

2. **Being with a message in a reflective state of wonder, awe, and adoration, say the authors, is when scripture and spiritual masters come alive for us. It is coming to know with the heart as we pierce through the knowledge gained by the logical intellect to another level. As we develop and deepen we begin to see in faith. As we begin to orient everything we say and do or think around the themes of committed living, we begin to wholly trust in the Lord, to remain simple in a complex world.**

    a. Read Psalm 95:1–7; 96:1–13; 97:1–12; 98:1–9; 99:1–9; 100:1–5. The writers of these psalms come before the Lord in wonder, awe, and adoration. Read each of them slowly. In Psalm 95:1–2, what transcendent disposition discussed in Part 5 occurs here? What is its source? In which other of these psalms is this disposition contained? What mention of light is there in Psalm 97? In which of these psalms are we referred to as the flock for which he tends?

    b. Read Revelation 4:1–11; 7:9–17. The future vision given to this writer shows the adoration of which the Lord is worthy. Who does verse 4:2 say inspired this vision? What are the prayers of adoration in Revelation verses 8 and 11? Are these familiar to you within your faith tradition? If so, where have you heard or said them before? In Revelation 7:16–17, what is received by those people dressed in the white robes?

c. Read Luke 4:16–21; Hebrews 4:12–13; 2 Timothy 3:14–17; 2 Peter 1:19–21. Seeing in faith begins as we open ourselves more and more to God's grace alive and at work in us. How does Jesus evidence the power of scripture speaking to him in his own life in the account in Luke? What do the writer of Hebrews, Paul in his letter to Timothy, and the writer of 2 Peter tell us about scripture? What has been your own experience with the word of God? Would you say that you approach it as if to become a servant or a master of the word? Which would God have us be—master or servant of the word? Recall a time when a passage of scripture may have come to life for you in a new way? What was the passage? What was the insight into scripture that you received? How did it speak to you in your everyday life?

d. Read Acts 8:26–38 and 1 Peter 3:15. How does the story of Philip and the Ethiopian official show that we are to continue growing in our understanding of God's word? In Acts 8:39, what effect does understanding the word have on the Ethiopian? What does Peter say we must be ready at all times to do?

e. Read Psalm 131. How does this prayer of humble trust illustrate the way to remain simple in a complex world? What has the person given up in verse 1? What disposition does the person experience in verse 2? Where is it experienced? What makes that possible? Reflect on the image of comfort in verse 2. What, if any, is the picture from your own experience that this image brings to mind?

3. **The authors tell us that prayer opens the door to the gift of divine transforming love awaiting us. In prayer, we should follow the way the Spirit leads and make room in our heart for the experience of God's loving presence deep within us and all around us. Jesus himself gave the example of remaining in God's presence by time and again creating moments of stillness in his life to be alone with God.**

a. Read Luke 6:12–16; 9:28–36; 11:1–13; Matthew 6:5–14. The gospel of Luke makes many references to Jesus' way of prayer. In Luke 6, we discover that Jesus prayed the whole night before making what important choices? In Luke 9, what happens in the midst of Jesus' praying? In Luke 11 and Matthew 6, Jesus teaches us how to pray. As you reflect on these words, try to imagine yourself hearing them for the first time as were the apostles. What might they have been thinking as they heard these words? In Matthew 6:5–7, how does Jesus tell us not to pray? Reflect on Matthew 6:8. How do you personally know this to be true? In Luke 11:13, what are we directed by Jesus to ask for in prayer?

b. Read Ephesians 6:13–20; 1 Thessalonians 5:16–17; Romans 8:26–28; 1 John 4:13–15. Paul teaches about prayer also in many of his letters. In Ephesians 6:17, what is the word of God compared to? Who gives this to us? When does verse 18 tell us that we are to pray? How are we to pray? What does 1 Thessalonians tell us about prayer? In Romans 8, who are we told pleads to God for us and teaches us how to pray? Recall a time when you had a brief glimpse of a presence beyond words. What was the situation? What words might you use to describe this experience? What message does John 1 share with us?

c. Read Matthew 14:22–27; Mark 1:35–38; Luke 5:15–16; Zechariah 2:13 [Zech 2:17 in some texts]; Psalm 46:10. How do the events of praying described in the three gospels show that Jesus needed the balance of stillness and time alone with God to keep his life oriented toward his deeper calling and commitment? Reflect on the word given to us by the prophet Zechariah and the writer of Psalm 46. What do those words say to your own heart?

RECORD YOUR DIALOGUE

ON YOUR OWN

Record that which touches your life, that which inspires you and deepens your awareness of your life direction in the light of your commitment to your own specific Christian faith and formation tradition.

IN THE GROUP

If your group has decided to allot a short time for notebook sharing, you may, if you wish, offer insights that might benefit the other members of the group.

RECLAIM THE CLASSICS

ON YOUR OWN
Read over the following annotated suggestions for further reading. Reflect on the glimpses given to see which classics you might like to "reclaim."

Anonymous. *The Cloud of Unknowing* and *The Book of Privy Counseling.* Ed. William Johnston. Garden City, N.Y.: Doubleday, Image Books, 1973.

This spiritual classic, written by an unknown director of souls, offers the reader a literary work of great beauty as well as a practical guide to the path of contemplation. The way to reach God is not through concepts but through love. God's mystery will always escape our analysis, but we can know in Christ just how near God is to us. In his treatise on "counseling" or private spiritual direction, the author describes the way to "enlightenment" through loss of one's ego-self. His goal is to instill in us a consciousness of God, however busy and distracted our lives may be.

Anonymous. *The Way of a Pilgrim* and *The Pilgrim Continues His Way.* Trans. R.M. French. New York: Crossroad, 1965.

This extraordinary account of the life of a pilgrim, a wanderer-in-Christ, brings the reader into the heart of eastern orthodox Christianity and the hesychast method of prayer, which centers on the words of the publican, "Lord Jesus Christ, Son of God, have mercy on me a sinner." The pilgrim practices "prayer without ceasing" according to a method whose efficacy has been proven by monks and laity alike. Calling on the name of Jesus, imploring his grace at all times, is a source of consolation and a sure way to conversion of heart.

Bloom, Anthony. *Living Prayer.* London: Darton, Longman & Todd, 1966.

The author's personal spirituality finds its roots in the eastern orthodoxy that holds that unless prayer is linked to action, it cannot bear fruit. He believes that our goal must be not only to say prayers but with our whole heart and mind to become living prayer.

Catherine of Siena. *The Dialogue*. Trans. Suzanne Noffke, O.P. New York: Paulist Press, 1980.

This soaring dialogue between a surrendered soul and a benevolent God shows the fruits of combining contemplation and action, knowledge and love. For Catherine, Christ is the only source of saving hope for our lives. To cultivate intimacy with God is not merely the goal of the mystic; it is the meaning of everyone's life.

Merton, Thomas. *Contemplative Prayer*. New York: Doubleday, Image Books, 1971.

This book represents the fruit of several decades of reflection and experience. In familiar, conversational style, Merton illumines the hard realities and upheavals of authentic prayer life as well as the joy, reverence, and expectation that inform it. Given the treasures of our formation tradition, the author is concerned about the spiritual inertia he sees in the contemporary Christians' disregard for the efficacy of ceaseless prayer. By combining personal experience with traditional knowledge, Merton guides the reader from superficial to profound prayer. He reaffirms his belief that all persons, not only those who live in monasteries, are invited by grace to be mindful of God. In a culture inclined to forget the depth of divine love, Merton challenges us not to separate the sacred and the secular but to become contemplatives in action.

Muto, Susan Annette. *Pathways of Spiritual Living*. Petersham, Mass.: St. Bede's Publications, 1984.

Grounded in scripture as well as in the teachings of the classical masters, this text aims to harmonize the collected wisdom of our Christian formation tradition with our contemporary search for intimacy with God amidst daily endeavors. The truth of our being present to God, open to grace, reconciled with one another, and called to holiness is beginning to dawn on a population far too long bent only on consumption and unfair competition. We are taken by the author through each step along the way of spiritual living: silence, formative reading, meditation, prayer, contemplation, and action. There is also in the book an excellent chapter on the discipline of keeping a spiritual journal, so that self-reflection accompanies self-donation.

Teresa of Avila, St. *The Way of Perfection.* Trans. E. Allison Peers. Garden City, N.Y.: Doubleday, Image Books, 1964.

St. Teresa's superb classic on the practice of prayer is addressed to all who are seeking a more perfect, that is to say, Godward way of life. She begins with an extensive treatment of the three essentials of a prayer-filled life—fraternal love, detachment from created things, and true humility, after which she offers her inspiring commentary on the Lord's Prayer. Throughout the text she sets forth livable directives for the attainment of graced transformation, a goal she assures us is within reach of any true disciple.

BRIEF GLOSSARY

The following glossary clarifies twenty terms used in this workbook. It articulates their meaning in the light of holy scripture. It offers an example of how the language of universal spiritual formation can point to the basic principles of committed Christian living outlined in this text.

1. ## *Abandonment Option*

To be formed in the image and likeness of God implies that we choose with Christ to surrender ourselves to the will of God as it is disclosed in our life and world. During his last agony Jesus prayed to his Father: ". . . if it is possible, let this cup pass me by. Still, let it be as you would have it, not as I" (Mt 26:39; see also Mt 6:10; 26:42; Mk 14:36; Lk 22:42; Jn 4:34; Heb 10:7, 9, 10).

In English the word "abandonment" or to "abandon" may connote some apathy or passivity. For this reason we connect the word "abandonment" with the word "option." Christian abandonment suggests, therefore, that we are free before God to make a decision, albeit with much struggle and uncertainty. We pray earnestly that what we decide will be in accordance with the mystery of God's will for us: "Rejoice always, never cease praying, render constant thanks; such is God's will for you in Christ Jesus" (1 Thes 5:16–18; see also Mt 7:21; Acts 21:12–14; Rom 12:2; Eph 5:17; Phil 2:5–8; Col 1:9–10; 1 Jn 2:17; 5:14).

2. ## *Affinity of Grace*

The word "affinity" means to be "alike" or to have a "likeness to." Hence "affinity of grace" means the slow and gradual disclosure over a lifetime of the image or form Christ wants to give to our life. "Just as we resemble the man from earth, so shall we bear the likeness of the man from heaven" (1 Cor 15:49; see also 2 Cor 3:18). The phrase can also refer to the likeness that a group open to God's grace shares. "The community of believers were of one heart and one mind" (Acts 4:32).

The Spirit endows us with the special graces that accompany this, our deepest call. Once we discover such an affinity, we are free to accept or refuse our unique call to likeness with Christ. But we can trust that in his graciousness God always wants in some way to draw us back to the unique image he meant for us from eternity. We are, therefore, to put aside our "old self" with its past deeds and put on a "new self," one that grows in knowledge as we are "formed anew in the image of [our] Creator" (Col 3:10).

3. *Appraisal*

To live in faithfulness to the image or form of Christ within us is to share in the praise of Christ offered to the Father and the Holy Spirit. "I offer you praise, O Father, Lord of heaven and earth, because what you have hidden from the learned and the clever you have revealed to the merest children" (Lk 10:21). In all that we choose to do, we must ask: Does this bring praise to God? Is it an offer of thanksgiving? Therefore, we have to ap-praise everything we receive and every act we perform in the light of the glory it gives to God. "Whatever you do, whether in speech or in action, do it in the name of the Lord Jesus. Give thanks to God the Father through him" (Col 3:17; see also 1 Cor 10:12–13, 31). In this sense a disposition (see #19) of appraisal is essential for committed Christian living.

4. *Appraisal Process*

Appraisal is not a one time act; it is a lifelong process. It includes different acts and dispositions, four of which are: attention, appreciation, affirmation, and application. We have to pay *attention* to the directives that come to us from daily life and from the Spirit; we have to *appreciate* that God has our best interest at heart (see #5 and #6). It is not enough merely to see a direction; we have to *affirm* this direction by an act of the will and to implement it in our life. Once we begin to *apply* our "yes" to God to daily living, we have to test out in reality how well this decision makes sense in relation to our other commitments: ". . . let us love in deed and in truth and not merely talk about it. This is our way of knowing we are committed to the truth and are at peace before [God] . . ." (1 Jn 3:18–20).

5. *Appreciation*

To appreciate means to place a value on something; for example, antiques "appreciate" in value as the years go by. Here the word is used to express that graced appreciation has the power to reveal to us the will of the Father. "Whatever you do, whether in speech or in action, do it in the name of the Lord Jesus. Give thanks to God the Father through him" (Col 3:17). Appreciative thinking also enables us to enjoy the wonderful epiphanies or manifestations of the Eternal in nature and in our everyday life. In other words our whole life becomes a quest to acknowledge: "How great are your works, O Lord!" (Ps 92:6).

6. *Appreciative Abandonment*

Once we are graced with an appreciation of God's presence in a situation, we become filled with joy and peace, fully abandoned to the mystery of God's love, the wisdom of his ways. "For my thoughts are not your thoughts, nor are your ways my ways, says the Lord. As high as the heavens are above the earth, so high are my ways above your ways, and my thoughts above your thoughts" (Is 55:8–9; see also Phil 4:4–7).

7. *Apprehension of Dissonance*

The word "dissonance" refers to those times when we are not in tune with the will of the Father in our life. We literally do not allow his will to "sound through" in our life. Another word for "being in tune" is consonance (see #10). This means literally to "sound together with" the formation mystery (see #13). It follows that the awareness of being "out of tune" with God's allowing will could be called dissonance, or what Timothy calls making a "shipwreck" of our faith (1 Tim 1:19).

Often sin blinds us to our unfaithfulness to the Christ-form (see #9); but at other times we have intimations, little flurries of fear or pinches of guilt, that may signify that our lives are no longer in conformity with God's graced promptings. "What happens is that I do, not the good I will do, but the evil I do not intend. But if I do what is against my will, it is not I who do it, but sin which dwells in me" (Rom 7:19–20). Essential for committed Christian living is our willingness to pay attention to these "apprehensions of dissonance."

8. *Aspirations*

These are graced movements of the human heart upward in response to inner spiritual promptings. The scriptures tell us of Christians expressing their longing for God in songs and hymns of thanksgiving (Ps 42:5 and Ps 63), of groaning with nature for redemption (Rom 8:23), of praying with sighs too deep for words (Rom 8:26). These graced movements differ essentially from the needs and drives of which human psychology speaks. They signify the longing of the human heart for "more than" mere functional accomplishment or vital gratification can attain.

9. *Christ-form*

Christians believe that through baptism they receive the image or form of Christ Jesus (Gal 3:27; 4:19). "He will give a new form to this lowly body of ours and remake it according to the pattern of his glorified body, by his power to subject everything to himself" (Phil 3:21). Over a lifetime Christians are called, in cooperation with God's grace, to allow this unique image of Christ within to give form to their entire life and world. "Let us not grow weary of doing good; if we do not relax our efforts, in due time we shall reap our harvest" (Gal 6:9).

10. *Consonance*

Consonance means in effect that we are on the same "wave length" as the Holy Spirit, that we experience a certain peace and joy, a feeling of being-together or integrated. In God alone will our soul "find rest" (Mt 11:29). The word reminds us of the "sonar" system that warns of pending obstacles and guides ships and planes to a safe landing. Consonance with the Holy Spirit assures us of coming home to God already during our pilgrimage through this life, for, as Jesus says, "In my Father's house there are many dwelling places" (Jn 14:2). When we listen to the word of God, God comes to us and enables us to make our dwelling place with him (Jn 14:23).

11. *Depreciation*

To depreciate means to devalue something—for example, out of envy to lessen the value of another's creativity. The demon of envy led to Cain killing his brother Abel (Gn 4:3–7) and to Joseph's brothers selling him into slavery in Egypt (Gn 37:5–7). Here the word depreciation has two meanings. First of all, we may develop a general disposition of depreciation that inclines us not to see the goodness of God shining forth in everyday life. Instead we lean in the direction of seeing the ugly or pointing out the unpleasant, depressing side of people, events and things. Such a disposition can create around us a climate of negativity. This makes it difficult for us to live in praise of the Father's will as Jesus did, even in his darkest hour (Mt 27:46).

The second type of depreciation has a good aim. We depreciate or devalue something in service of coming to more appreciation. If we have wisely appraised what God asks of us in our here and now situation, we can rightly depreciate whatever hinders this divine direction. As Paul says: ". . . those things I used to consider gain I have now reappraised as loss in the light of Christ. I have come to rate all as loss in the light of the surpassing knowledge of my Lord Jesus Christ. For his sake I have forfeited everything; I have accounted all else rubbish so that Christ may be my wealth . . ." (Phil 3:7–8).

12. *Depreciative Abandonment*

This term means that instead of abandoning ourselves *to* God's love and mercy, we feel abandoned *by* God. We are inclined to see only how hopeless things are, how meaningless any form of suffering is. This experience that we are "thrown," as it were, into an uncaring universe, subject to suffering and death without the loving embrace of God, can lead to low-grade depression and a feeling that life is disintegrating under our eyes. It can breed cynicism or even suicidal despair. Hence, the psalmist cries: "Save me, O God, for the waters threaten my life; I am sunk in the abysmal swamp where there is no foothold; I have reached the watery depths; the flood overwhelms me. I am wearied with calling, my throat is parched; my eyes have failed with looking for my God" (Ps 69:2–4).

13. *Formation Mystery*

The word "mystery" refers to the scriptural idea that we cannot make false idols of God and that we can never totally grasp with our finite human minds what God is (Dt 5:6–10). The divine life of the Holy Trinity is and remains for us a mystery. The expression "formation mystery" reminds us that the form God is giving to our life in Christ Jesus is also a mystery (Phil 2:5–7). It will only be disclosed to us in part over a lifetime, for ". . . what we shall later be has not yet come to light" (1 Jn 3:2).

The divine form meant for us by God far surpasses any psychological knowledge of human developmental stages or sociocultural influences. "How deep are the riches and the wisdom and the knowledge of God! How inscrutable his judgments, how unsearchable his ways!" (Rom 11:33). For this reason scripture never speaks of "human development" but repeatedly mentions the form God gives to our life and world: "Truly you have formed my inmost being; you knit me in my mother's womb" (Ps 139:13; see also Is 43:1, 7; 44:2, 24; 49:5).

14. *Inspirations*

These are gifts of counsel granted by the Holy Spirit that surpass mere psychological intuitions and insights. Scripture tells us that the Holy Spirit works in us: "Who, for example, knows a man's innermost self but the man's own spirit within him? Similarly, no one knows what lies at the depths of God but the Spirit of God. The Spirit we have received is not the world's spirit but God's Spirit, helping us recognize the gifts he has given us" (1 Cor 2:11–12; see also Jn 14:25).

15. *Mystery of Transforming Love*

This mystery is rooted in the revelation that God has loved us first (1 Jn 4:10) and that God never withdraws his love from us. His love makes us a new creation, or, what is the same, transforms us (Eph 2:10; 4:24). Experience teaches us that all forms of life, however committed and beautiful they may be, can be impermanent and transitory. The only thing we can be sure of is that God's love lasts forever (see Ps 89:2; 106:1; 136:1; Jer 31:3). This belief transforms our hearts and lives. The eternal love of God for us never leaves us orphaned (Is 49:15–16); it never betrays us, no matter how limited and poor we are. We cannot fathom the depth of God's gracing love. It is overwhelming, awesome. If we believe in this great mystery and live with it intimately, our lives will change, our commitments will deepen, our charity will increase. "There are in the end three things that last: faith, hope, and love, and the greatest of these is love" (1 Cor 13:13).

16. *Pneumatic*

The Greek term "pneuma" (Acts 2:4) refers to the third person of the Blessed Trinity. Hence the adjective refers to the working in our human spirit of the Holy Spirit (Acts 2:38). Many so-called "new age spiritualities" and "transpersonal psychologies" dwell on what it means to cultivate the "God"-like qualities of the human spirit. Some even go so far as to suggest that our human spirit is God. Against such pantheistic tendencies, scripture insists that the human spirit has to be transformed and elevated beyond its pride and sinfulness by the Holy Spirit whom Jesus promised us (see Jn 14:16–17; 14:26; Jn 15:26).

We cannot hope to attain the unique image and form of Christ to which we are called on the basis of our human spirits alone. Faith in the saving power of Jesus through the Holy Spirit, not works alone, is the key to our divine transformation (see Rom 5:1–5; 2 Cor 5:17; Eph 4:24; Col 3:10). Therefore, "The kingdom of God is not a matter of eating or drinking, but of justice, peace, and the joy that is given by the Holy Spirit. Whoever serves Christ in this way pleases God and wins the esteem of [all]" (Rom 14:17–18).

17. *Pride-form*

Baptized Christians are called to live in the image and likeness of God in Jesus Christ: "All who are led by the Spirit of God are sons [and daughters] of God. You did not receive a spirit of slavery leading you back in fear, but a spirit of adoption through which we cry out 'Abba!' . . . The Spirit himself gives witness with our spirit that we are children of God" (Rom 8:14–16). However, original sin counters this call; it inclines us since the fall of humankind to live in the image of what we want to be independently of grace.

Autonomous self-fulfillment seduces us from the awareness of our dependence on the saving power of our Lord Jesus Christ (Rom 5:11; see also 2 Cor 4:7). When we succumb to this inclination, we obscure the image or form of Christ in us. Instead we take on a counterfeit pride-form that tempts us to believe that we can give a perfect form to our life by our own powers alone. We may fall victim to seductive projects of self-salvation, suggesting that we alone or with others can, by means of certain "spiritual" practices or disciplines, save or redeem ourselves. "See to it that no one deceives you through any empty, seductive philosophy that follows mere human traditions, a philosophy based on cosmic powers rather than on Christ" (Col 2:8; see also Heb 3:1–19; Eph 4:17–19; Tit 2:11–14).

18. *Pseudo-spiritual Pragmatism*

One way in which the pride form operates is to make us invest in practical accomplishments the whole meaning of life—to make functional effectiveness or financial success the basis of our belief. These projects, achievements, and pragmatic accomplishments may be seen as "spiritual" or virtuous in themselves. One may be motivated solely by self-centered and worldly concerns. In this case one's spiritual life is not rooted in transcendent dispositions but in power-seeking, possessive, or only pleasurable ways of life. But all the goods the world has to offer do not guarantee happiness. We must grow rich in the sight of God and avoid greed in all its forms (Lk 12:13–21).

19. *Transcendent Dispositions*

During the course of a lifetime, we cultivate many dispositions. Some may be lasting, like trust; others passing, like the stamina needed to find a new job. Some dispositions are pre-transcendent. These would include gratification in the realm of pleasure or satisfaction in the realm of functional accomplishment. With the aid of grace, we may be formed in dispositions that are the fruit of God's transforming love in our life (see #15). This love enables us to go beyond or transcend merely secular or selfish concerns and to grow instead in patience and peace, wisdom and fortitude, and other gifts of the Holy Spirit (see 1 Cor 14:1; Gal 5:22–23; 1 Thes 5:14–15).

20. *Transcendent Essence*

What we are essentially in the eyes of God goes beyond anything we can do or observe in our everyday existence. We are, in other words, more than what day to day living or accomplishment can suggest. Our basic call, essence, or form of life is hidden in Christ and Christ is hidden in God (1 Cor 3:23; Col 1:27; 3:3). This deepest aspect of who we are from all eternity in the mind of God can only be seen with the eyes of faith. We cannot grasp our deepest unique essence in God. We cannot observe or measure it by means of any text or personality inventory. We are and remain a mystery even to ourselves. This unique essence that we are in God's loving heart goes beyond what any human psychology can analyze. "Of this wisdom it is written: 'Eye has not seen, ear has not heard, nor has it so much as dawned on man what God has prepared for those who love him'" (1 Cor 2:9).